First Survivor
The Impossible Childhood Cancer Breakthrough

Mark Unger

This is not a medical journal nor a how-to guide.
Always consult with medical professionals for any medical needs. This book is a true story of our unique journey.

To find out more about this book, see videos of the family discussing their journey and other information please visit the website at www.first-survivor.com.

All proceeds from this book will go to the Carrot Seed Foundation founded by Mary Ellen and Mark Unger where they will be used to fund Neuroblastoma clinical trials and support the children and families who are stricken by this disease.

Please visit www.carrotseedfoundation.org for more information.

DEDICATION

I dedicate this book to Mary Ellen, Harry, and Louis.

To Louis, who fought this battle with an unrelentingly positive attitude and true grit. He motivated everyone around him to do the same. How a boy so young was able to endure so much is a miracle. A true warrior.

To Harry, who always loved and supported his brother. Harry was always there to play, pray, and be Louis's best friend. He was our anchor at home. The best big brother on earth.

To my amazing wife. I am truly a lucky man. She protected, fed, cleaned, medicated, educated, laughed, and cried with Louis 24/7 while taking care of Harry and me as well. My angel.

Mary Ellen, Harry and Louis you are a constant source of strength, joy and pride. Our love for each other got us through..

FOREWORD

This book chronicles the suffering, despair, and ultimate triumph of the Unger family in overcoming a deadly pediatric cancer called neuroblastoma. Faced with desperate situations, his loving family was determined to save his young life by reaching out to friends and the internet to search for expertise in novel cancer therapies. Throughout this arduous journey, and without any guarantee of success, they have courageously walked into the unknown. Louis was indeed a trail blazer in the then untested clinical study, which has now proven to help many other children afflicted with neuroblastoma that has spread to the brain. We all salute the Ungers for their courage.

Nai-Kong V. Cheung, MD, PhD
Head, Neuroblastoma Program;
Enid A. Haupt Chair in Pediatric Oncology
Memorial Sloan Kettering Cancer Center

PREFACE

Our son's battle with childhood cancer changed everything for my family. Sharing our story brings all the difficult emotions flooding back, but I believe it's a journey worth describing because it might help others. This book shows how my family cried, laughed, and rode the scariest roller coaster imaginable.

Our son's survival became an obsession. We learned it was ultimately up to us to protect our son and to find the best path for his survival. Louis, who was three when first diagnosed, showed the unrelenting courage and determination of a true warrior. He gave us the strength to confront and reject the diagnosis of "Zero chance of survival."

I hope this book honors our extended family, friends, and the dedicated doctors who ultimately made the difference between life and death for our son. My message is this: There are no dead ends, only new paths.

This is not a medical journal or a how-to guide. It is a real-life thriller that gives you a front row seat to a miraculous story of courage and determination.

ACKNOWLEDGEMENTS

This book was made possible by the compassion and love of my wife. Despite Mary Ellen's pain of reliving this story, she worked by my side to recount her deep memories and emotions. It was a monumental task and I am forever grateful she did it to help me complete my dream of writing this book. I love this woman.

My deep gratitude goes to the incredible pediatric oncologists who helped guide us through the many phases of Louis's treatment. Dr. Brian Kushner cared deeply for Louis and led his treatment at Sloan Kettering. He was instrumental in seeing a medical path that had never been tried before to save our son's life. We will forever be grateful to him as he enjoys receiving pictures of Louis's path in life.

Thanks to Dr. Nai-Kong V. Cheung, who founded and leads the Neuroblastoma Department at Sloan Kettering for inventing the lifesaving 3F8 antibodies. His mission is to cure this terrible cancer and his work remains at the leading edge of its treatment. We remain in awe of his fearless pursuit of new treatments to save our kids.

Our deep gratitude goes to Dr. Kim Kramer who led the intrathecal protocol that saved Louis's life. She guided us through this phase of treatment and made the experience less frightening than it was.

We want to thank the incredibly gifted surgeons who were able to remove the deadly tumors from our son's body and brain without harming anything around them. Dr. La Quaglia and Dr. Souwadeine are gifts to all the children they have saved.

Thanks to all the nurses who spent countless hours tending to our son's every need. We are forever in debt to your around-the-clock dedication. The love and caring the nurses had for Louis helped us get through many difficult times.

Many thanks go to Anne Delaney, Mary Ellen's mother and Barbara Unger Wales, my mother, who took care of Harry whenever needed. They were both always there for us and without them our mission would have been impossible.

I am also grateful to my brothers, Jan and Dane, who allowed me to take a leave of absence from our business to be there 100% for my family.

I also wish to thank all the other caregivers, doctors, surgeons and professionals who helped care for Louis during his years of treatments.

A big thank you to Michael Strouch who was able to change our medical insurance so we could go to Sloan Kettering.

I also wish to acknowledge with gratitude the role played by Frank Delaney in the creation of this book. Thanks also go to Annabelle Howard for her editorial and technological expertise.

A big thank you goes to Make-A-Wish of Connecticut for making Lou's wish "to dig for dinosaurs" come true.

CONTENTS

Unger family portrait. Fall 2000. Louis is 2 ½ years old.

Harry and Louis in the Badlands of SD. August 2001.

CHAPTER 1: DAY ONE

It all began toward the end of August 2001, when my wife, Mary Ellen, began to notice that our younger child was suddenly walking in a strange way. Three-year-old Louis was kicking out his right leg to the side as he took a step. It wasn't a limp, but his right foot now turned out a little when he walked.

Always a quieter child than his older brother Harry, Louis had also been growing less talkative, Mary Ellen confided to me. Once she had pointed this out, I immediately saw it was true. This new style of walking and his growing silence worried us both.

Louis was already a solid baby when he was born. His hands were meaty like a catcher's mitt and his body was as strong as his hands. He was a very happy child growing up, always laughing and smiling at the world around him. As he grew from baby to toddler he was a joy, always wanting to play outside and explore new frogs and insects.

He had already developed a stubborn side with this otherwise sunshine personality. It was a well- known family trait my wife would remind me. When he did not get what he wanted—look out! He loved to play with Harry who was two years older. They were best friends and were often having fun or getting in trouble together.

Any sudden or dangerous drop in a child's physical or mental responses, any unexpected impairment, and any departure from a busy and inquisitive daily routine sets off alarm in a parent's heart and soul. My wife took Louis to his pediatrician, Dr. Gregory Germain, twelve miles away, in New Haven, Connecticut, home of the Yale School of Medicine.

Dr. Germain promptly referred Louis Unger, our precious three-year-old boy, to a **pediatric orthopedist** named Dr. Tom Renshaw, who was also Professor Emeritus of Orthopaedics and Rehabilitation at the Yale School of Medicine. After physical examinations and **X-rays**, the two doctors agreed on a **diagnosis**: Perthes disease."

Legg-Calvé-Perthes, a rare ailment, afflicts young children by way of an interrupted blood flow to the hip socket, and its presence shows in the crooked way they walk. It may need treatment, up to and including orthopedic surgery. Or, in time, they can grow out of it; neither direction is unusual. Fifty children in a million suffer from it between the ages of three and ten, it's half a dozen times more common in boys than girls, and it's often confused with or dismissed as "growing pains," especially in an active child such as Louis Unger.

Once they had conferred, and agreed on Perthes, Dr. Germain was convinced that the **prognosis** was very sound, and we had a game plan which gave us some peace of mind.

However, both doctors would be blindsided by the speed and viciousness of what was to come—a different and somewhat rare diagnosis that Dr. Germain to this day has only seen twice in his life, a disease that offers slim hope of recovery.

On September 11, the same day as the attacks on the World Trade Center in New York City, and a week or so after this initial examination, Louis Unger began attending our local nursery school in Bethany, a few minutes from our Connecticut home. My wife shared our concerns with the Director of the nursery school, Pat Garcia, explaining that Louis might have "this Perthes syndrome." We all agreed to be extra vigilant.

It didn't take long for Mrs. Garcia to report that Louis seemed "maybe out of it a little." Mary Ellen was meticulous about communicating with Mrs. Garcia each day, and then keeping me in the loop. Louis seemed to not quite have the stamina he used to exhibit.

Before long, Mary Ellen observed something new; Louis was going back to taking naps in the afternoon, when by all toddler norms he should no longer need to sleep during the day. For the time being, we explained this away by understanding it to be part of an adjustment to the higher activity demands of nursery school, compared with being at home.

As October replaced September, Mary Ellen observed a fourth change. Louis had not only been slowing down, he had also been getting more irritable to the point of downright anger. Normally a sweet and affectionate boy, he had now made a few harsh and uncharacteristic remarks, such as, "Why don't you go off to where the war men are and get killed like all those other people?" These words were spoken in the direct aftermath of 9/11. We realized that Louis must be significantly distressed, and yet we had no way of discovering the root cause for sure, because a three- year-old can't say why he's feeling so unhappy.

Although we tried to console each other, we both felt a creeping helplessness and panic. Our little son had an ailment that was now affecting his mood and his life in general. We couldn't make him better with a hug and a kiss. Alarm swept in like a tide.

When Louis began to complain that his left leg was also hurting, Mary Ellen took him back to the pediatric orthopedist, Dr. Tom Renshaw, who immediately took a follow-up X-ray—that was on the Monday of

Thanksgiving week, 2001. Mary Ellen also made an appointment to see the pediatrician, Dr. Germain, not the next day, but on Wednesday—to give Louis an extra day with his new friends at nursery school.

When Dr. Renshaw read the X-rays he reached a different opinion. It is over a decade since all this took place, yet his colleague, Dr. Germain, still has a vivid recollection of receiving the new diagnosis from his colleague. At that time, Dr. Germain was in his early thirties and he had a son the same age as Louis. This made us feel he identified closely with our intense feelings of urgency and need for resolution. A dozen years later, he still has an inches-high file of papers on this case sitting in his office.

"Routine follow-up with routine X-rays. Yes, that's typical, that's what you do. And then, right before Thanksgiving - that's when the horror was uncovered. In follow-up, he [the orthopedist] had done his usual films, and there were some horrifyingly wrong things going on," Dr. Germain told us, years later.

He added: "I was in one of our satellite offices, and I was sitting in the back room when I received the phone call from Tom Renshaw and he told me that he had concerns. He was disturbed that in the follow-up he had seen some obvious abnormalities on the X-ray—some lesions on the bone that were very unusual.

"Pediatrics—it's newborns, it's happy moms. But these are the cases that you have nightmares about," Dr. Germain said, much later.

My wife and I, like all married couples, divide our family responsibilities. I normally go to my office each day and she normally took the children to doctors' visits whenever they were needed. However, with all her instincts firing, Mary Ellen asked me to take Wednesday morning off so that we could take Louis to the doctor together. She got five-year-old Harry onto the school bus, and then I drove the three of us to the pediatrician in New Haven. When Dr. Germain walked into his office at nine o'clock we were waiting for him.

Gregory Germain is a seasoned, calm and engaging man. It is obvious he has committed his soul to the medical care of children, and relishes his work. He lights up when he speaks of the privilege the universe has given him, the gift of improving young lives. He's also an organized individual, there's no trace of dishevelment in his office or his person. He's a cheerful and relaxed man, tidy, well-geared for life in general, and for his profession in particular. He is most reassuring.

When he walked into his office that morning, the first thing he saw was Louis, low in vitality, resting on the examination table. Dr. Germain dropped the folder of X-rays he was carrying. A mishap from an organized man might well indicate a sense of disturbance, and Gregory Germain's momentary and uncharacteristic clumsiness did speak volumes—he had dreadful news to share. The blood tests taken at the same time as the recent X-rays were showing what he called—for the moment "extreme anemia," meaning low blood counts, low energy, and a lack of oxygen that would produce lethargy. With kindness and urgency, he insisted we go to the Children's Emergency Room at Yale-New Haven Hospital, where he would meet us immediately. My wife and I looked at each other and then we both looked at Louis in total silence.

Years after our ordeal was over, Dr. Germain confided the following to me: "When you're discussing a horrible diagnosis you have to walk a fine line, it takes a lot of sensitivity and tact. On the other hand, you know that as soon as the cat is out of the bag, parents hear nothing more of what you say. So you have to be sensitive and concise, and really be prepared ahead of time to have the discussion and answer the questions. And, most importantly, to have the next step worked out. You don't want to say, 'This is horrible, now I have to figure out what to do.' You really need to lead, and show some guidance."

Dr. Germain's office was only a few blocks from Yale-New Haven hospital; however, New Haven has a one-way system of roads. I drove the complex patterns, making turn after turn, while Louis innocently cuddled with Mary Ellen in the back seat. We arrived at the Children's **ER**, soon after ten o'clock. Before long, in a small and nondescript room a parade of doctors made short visits, stared hard at Louis, smiled at us weakly and said almost nothing— never a good sign. Dr. Germain soon joined us in silence. We feared some unspeakably awful thing and had no words either, just terrifying thoughts. In the vacuum without information the mind always seems to go to the darkest places.

Before long, Dr. Germain left us alone. We sat and we sat. The little room had a little television. Louis watched Bob the Builder while Mary Ellen and I watched our dear little, unsuspecting boy. More doctors came by, peered, poked, and left. Given the no-nonsense urgency with which we had been directed to the ER, the increasing listlessness of our child, and the screaming anxiety rising within us, even a short delay felt like forever. If the fire of fear hadn't been torching us, we might have been able to correctly assume that the hospital doctors, alerted by Dr. Germain, were re-examining the X-rays.

In time, our pediatrician returned, attended by a Child Life Specialist.

Descended tangentially from the early twentieth-century innovative educator, Maria Montessori, we soon understood that a Child Life Specialist trains in, among other things, pediatric education, child psychology, and trauma therapy.

Nurses began prepping Louis for an **intravenous** line in his arm to transfuse blood. Using a little doll, the Child Life Specialist showed Louis what they were about to do. Mary Ellen and I watched, understanding the placing of the IV line but not yet knowing why our three-year-old needed a blood transfusion.

And still the medical faces came, looked thoughtful, and then left. For hours, we held our breath and watched Bob the Builder. It was a welcomed distraction.

I know now that even in the best hospitals a reluctance to declare or explain anything at this point in their diagnosis is standard practice. Doctors do not discuss an ailment until all the facts have been gathered, a diagnosis confirmed, and treatment plan has been developed.

Prompted by anxiety and a mother's instinct, Mary Ellen began asking for answers. The hospital staff explained our lack of answers by saying, "It's Thanksgiving. People are away." Then, a new ER doctor arrived to take a look. She came in alone and unannounced, and when the pediatrician and the Child Life Specialist had gone, she was the only other person in the room with us. Mary Ellen asked her what was wrong with Louis and said she hadn't been getting any answers. "Just please tell us," begged my wife.

The ER doctor, after some hesitation, yielded to the anguished force of a mother's question and said that Louis possibly had **cancer**, probably **leukemia**, and that somebody would soon answer all our queries.

We knew it was going to be bad, but we were not prepared for her words. It is hard to describe the emotions at that moment—shock pain, anger, guilt, love—they swirled in our minds like tornadoes. What did she say? Cancer? Leukemia? Mary Ellen and I feared this news, and hearing it spoken made a dark fog of confusion emerge along with an immediate fear of the unknown. Little did we know how hard it would be to hold onto stable emotions during the years ahead.

After a few minutes, Mary Ellen and I regained some composure by hugging and kissing Louis. He was happily watching Bob on TV, oblivious to what was happening. We looked at each other and knew in that instant, we must push our emotions aside and focus on Louis—his life was at stake. Our three year-old innocent, adorable, loving son was under full attack and the enemy was winning.

Instinctively, my wife and I adopted roles that we held to through much of this catastrophe and we behaved perhaps as people do in a War Room—we kept going and did what we felt we must. Mary Ellen focused on Louis and tried to lessen the distress of his first-ever grave medical condition and treatments. She distracted him when nurses punctured his tender skin. She responded to his curiosity about the intravenous line. She minimized the risk of his sudden child movements pulling out a needle or bending a tube. At the same time, she took on the management of our family's day. She made sure Harry got home from school safely. She deftly adjusted our plans for tomorrow which was Thanksgiving.

My own coping mechanism was to start documenting everything in writing. I felt the urge to take notes—by hand that morning, and later on my laptop. This was the beginning of many years of detailed note-taking. In retrospect, I suppose it was a concrete action I could take that made me feel less helpless. Having a go-to activity at all times was reassuring and gave me the comforting illusion of having a little control in this nightmare. At any time, night or day, we were inundated with information that felt alien in words and meaning. Taking the time to write it down allowed us to create some solid ground that we could inspect and inhabit in our own time.

Learning and remembering so much information all at once was near impossible and I soon realized that if we were to survive, we had to understand the new world we had been thrown into very quickly.

At first, I had no system, no rules, no conscious plan and clearly my notes reflect the sense of chaos I felt. Here is a sample from Day One:

My first page of notes. Nov. 21, 2001.

November 21:

*Day before Thanksgiving 2001 >>Dr. Germain visit > X-Rays and anemia are signs for leukemia > Yale ER > test for blood cell counts & chest X-ray. Met Dr. Beardsley the Attending Oncologist/Hematologist and veteran at kids' leukemia > Prognosis – leukemia likely, bone **marrow** biopsy needed as cancer has not spread to blood. Acute anemia (5 instead of normal 12) > Round Table with Dr. Beardsley to discuss Lou's condition. Made aware of likely prognosis, types of cancer & treatment. 2 types possible 80% chance of A.L.L. which is 90% curable, 20% chance of A.M.L. which is only 50% curable. Needs immediate transfusion. Treatment – chemotherapy. A.L.L. = 1 week hospital: A.M.L. = 4 weeks hospital > Have child wellness counselors show Louis what the procedures will be like on dolls. Met Dr. Beardsley a resident and veteran*

8

at kids' leukemia.

Naturally, my wife and I wanted the very best for our child and this included the best doctors. We found ourselves assessing each doctor immediately and looking for doctors who had both superior professional track records as well as superior people skills. Dr. Diana Beardsley came across as a comforting presence; kind, direct and thoughtful, open, concerned but not over-emotional.

My wife remarked to me, "She is like your grandma. I'm sure she is not that much older than me, but she is a very calm person, respectful. And she listens deeply. I feel she sees me."

In other words, an unusual combination of natural creativity, medical attentiveness and attractive willpower came together in this humane woman. Greg Germain worked alongside Dr. Beardsley often, knew her well and later on he told me:

"Diana was a world-famous **hematologist**. She was probably the national expert on **clotting** disorders, **platelet** function. **Oncology** was not her first love, but she happened to be on call right before the holiday. And Diana was a loving, caring, big- hearted person. I think she was a fantastic physician but despite her gifts, oncology wasn't the central part of her job, she didn't focus on it every day. She was, in principle, hematology. World-renowned for it, and rightly so."

In those first hours on Wednesday afternoon, Dr. Beardsley dictated the earliest moves on the basis of a leukemia diagnosis and severe **anemia**—hence the need for that urgent blood transfusion. Her opinion inclined toward **A.L.L.**, Acute Lymphocytic Leukemia, rather than the significantly more threatening **A.M.L.**, Acute Myeloid Leukemia (also known as acute myelogenous leukemia). There was, she explained, a sixty per cent difference between them in the likelihood of a cure.

Both A.M.L. and A.L.L. deliver symptoms that Louis had been experiencing—tiredness, abdominal swelling, weakness, aches and pains in the bones or joints, a touch of fever.

It was neither A.L.L. nor A.M.L.

Mary Ellen and I had questions for Dr. Beardsley, in particular regarding the intravenous line for **transfusions** and chemotherapy. In her answers we heard the first of many ironies. With a growing child, when the body's system has enormous power for its age, cancer can develop rapidly. This is obviously not good. However, the same **metabolic** speed that drives the illness can be a remarkable advantage when it comes to chemotherapy—which can also travel fast when driven by a young metabolism. That is to say, in certain circumstances the body grants the same pace to the cure as to the disease.

While Dr. Beardsley and her team gave us their real diagnosis, the gravity of the situation started to sink in. Our emotions were in relative check after we left Bob the Builder behind in the ER. Now they came flooding back again—disbelief and the feeling of being overwhelmed that comes with acute stress.

Trauma victims and post-traumatic stress sufferers report the dominance of one fierce question: Is there nothing the world can do to give me peace? I remember experiencing a recurring mental image of riding a roller coaster. As I pictured myself in my mind's eye I literally felt anticipation, fear, relief, and free fall. The emotional comfort of my day-to-day life had evaporated and been replaced by constant panic. I didn't know it yet, but I would be riding that imaginary, relentless machine for two, three, and, finally, four awful years.

Meanwhile, Mary Ellen continued in practical mode: she called a neighbor to get Harry off the school bus. Shortly afterward, in the early evening, she left the hospital to pick up Harry from our neighbor's house, go home, and pack an overnight bag for herself.

"It was the first time that I was not at the bus when he got off, and I was concerned it would add to his anxiety if I weren't the parent to pick him up. I also wanted to prep him for seeing Louis in the hospital. As hard as it was to leave Louis, I really felt that Harry needed me more in that moment," Mary Ellen reported some time after this ordeal.

Once surrounded by the softer environment of home, she made a decision to give each of our boys an early Christmas present. Ironically, she had already purchased what Louis had previously asked for—a toy ambulance. She then brought Harry to the hospital to see his brother.

After dinner, my wife and I switched roles. I went home with Harry. Mary Ellen slept on a cramped vinyl couch in the room to which they had moved Louis in the children's hospital—the first of several hundred such nights that she would spend enduring discomfort and racking worry under a hospital roof. But at least that evening she could watch the color coming back into her son's face when they transfused the red blood cells.

As the night deepened, I could not sleep.

Instead, I wrote my last observations on the day that changed our lives forever:

Lou is opening up a little, had a good two-thirds small pizza for dinner. Lou & Harry play and watch TV. Dad and Harry go home at 9.00. Bed 9.30 with Harry & Daddy. Louis is getting his first transfusion of red blood cells tonight. Should make him feel better. Tomorrow is the marrow biopsy. We should know more by the afternoon.

CHAPTER 2: DAY TWO

On Thursday, November 22, 2001, the hospital corridors echoed stark and empty due to the alleged holiday. To find out what kind of beast this cancer might truly be, Dr. Beardsley had ordered a bone marrow **biopsy**; however, it was Thanksgiving Day, and nobody could find an **anesthesiologist**, and therefore no worthwhile anesthetic could be administered to Louis other than something mild and local along with some gentle, oral sedation.

A bone marrow biopsy needle, even in pediatric medicine, is several inches long, with a reception cradle to gather what is extracted. It has a depth stop to prevent it from going too far into the bone. In adult medicine, the pain is legendary. Louis was three years and ten months old.

In a room not much bigger than a small closet, he lay on his side and his mother sat opposite him. As the huge needle, a giant's weapon to a small boy, went into his pelvis, they played their favorite guessing games: I'm thinking of an animal? Is it a mammal? Yes, it's a mammal. Is it a giraffe? No, it's not a giraffe. I could not have loved my wife and son more at that moment.

Since only one parent was allowed to be present, Harry and I were swiftly escorted downstairs to a waiting area. During that searing bone-marrow procedure, which makes grown adults blanch in advance even if they know they will have a hefty anesthetic, something remarkable materialized something we couldn't have predicted, something that would prove a powerful gift. Louis showed a remarkable, close-to-unreal capacity for being the perfect patient. Stoic, enduring, cheerful, playful, steadfast beyond his years, he reacted as minimally as he could to the procedure. He fought to be a good boy; he waited for the breath-stopping shock of the needle to pass; he continued between gasps to play I'm Thinking of Something—Is it an elephant, Mom? No, it's not an elephant.

This procedure had serious importance. Once the biopsy results came back, Dr. Beardsley had said, chemotherapy would, in all likelihood, begin.

Here are some of my notes from Day Two:

November 22:
Hard Day for us > Louis starts procedure late at 10.15:
*Perhaps cancer **tumor** that has gone to marrow? Not A.L.L*

– may be a tumor, maybe A.M.L – not rule out rare type perhaps. Ultrasound today to look at kidney – perhaps a mass near kidney. Dr. Seashore pediatric surgeon to place IV central line.

*Enough cancer cells in marrow to test type of tumor. May need CAT or **bone scan** to determine. Urine collection for next 24 hours – last done for 12 hours. CAT scan scheduled for midnight to look for tumor. IV Central tomorrow – full anesthesia.*

Mary Ellen and I listened as the medical team ranged over and back across a minefield of possibilities. Maybe there's a tumor, maybe not? Did Dr. Beardsley's physical exam yield a **mass** near a kidney? If there's a tumor, the bone marrow biopsy will confirm and define it. Somebody mentioned the possibility of a rare type of cancer. They'll take another urine test, scan to look for a tumor, and establish another IV line tomorrow.

Just as tsunamis generally consist of a series of waves that sweep through a landscape in intervals ranging from minutes to hours, so did the medical news repeatedly swirl around us until we felt in danger of drowning. The fact that it was Thanksgiving felt impossible. Our family, like most American families loved Thanksgiving. Mary Ellen's plans had been made long in advance. The four of us were to go to my sister-in-law's house. Instead of this, my sister-in-law and other family members started arriving in Louis's room at Yale New Haven Hospital that Thursday evening. We wanted to let our immediate family know of our situation and knew we could all use all the love and support around us right now. They had the emotional smarts to take things easy, the commonsense to boost Louis's spirits, and the kind understanding required to maintain a sense of pleasant quiet in the face of whatever might have been burning inside them.

Mary Ellen reminded me that amid "All the painful things and the constant parade of doctors and residents and nurses—there was eating Thanksgiving dinner with my family in the playroom. They sent it up, from I-don't-know-where. Just big aluminum trays, mashed potatoes, corn, and turkey.

"We had our boys—and then there was a little boy who was in for treatment, and his folks weren't there, so he came and he ate with us. He missed his parents and being part of a family. I think he was only about eight years old, so young to be all alone for Thanksgiving, my heart just went out to him. Including him was a small way to make him feel like part of a family."

Some years later, in fourth grade, Harry wrote a school essay about that Thanksgiving Day in 2001 which went as follows:

> "When I saw Louis after that first day in the hospital, the fear began to gnaw at the back of my mind. I'd never seen my little brother like this and it scared me. My mom told me Lou was really sick, and very tired, and that I couldn't roughhouse with him like I usually did, and everyone would have to be very gentle with him.
>
> "The car ride from the hospital on Thanksgiving still hangs clear in my mind. The deserted streets of New Haven were surreal in their own right, and the brave face my parents had put on began to crack. Their profiles were swept across the seats by the passing street lights, and in their faces, puffy eyes offset determined features as each kept their real thoughts to themselves. Still scared by Louis's condition seeing my parents' own worry truly frightened me.
>
> "However, alongside our fear was a small nugget of hope and determination. My five-year-old self must have only seen it in the focus with which my dad was driving, or the look in my mom's eyes. I felt their strength drain my fear, and I knew from then on we were going to fight whatever had gotten my little brother sick."

By the second night, my wife and I had a new and unspoken system for living as a family. Mary Ellen's primary focus was to continue mothering Louis. This included monitoring and noting everything that happened to him. She charted the day and date of every needle and chemical, drug name and dosage that went into our son's body. This freed me up to ask question after question. I scoured the real world and the online world for wisdom from others who had faced this creature called "neuroblastoma."

When faced with hugely stressful situations in a foreign world, the best attempts at remaining even- tempered and cooperative make all the difference. If you openly panic, lose your cool, or try to mentally escape you will invite chaos into your life.

My life had always been organized and structured and I prided myself on overcoming obstacles. I enjoyed new experiences and challenges, always believing I could master what was ahead. Growing up in Solingen, Germany, where my mother and father started their business and moving to the U.S. at age twelve taught me how to adapt to a new culture, language, and life. After college, I worked in Japan for eight months and travelled the globe for our family business. Nothing fazed me. I could land anywhere in the world and know I would be ok.

I was not ok now. My normal sense of control was completely shattered. While Mary Ellen did all she could to help Louis, I was trying to find my footing. I knew I was no match for this world as I could not even understand the hospital language around me. In that moment, I was determined to shake off the feeling of despair inside me. I had to be strong even if inside I felt the opposite.

CHAPTER 3: DAY THREE

Day three of this nightmare happened on Friday, November 23, and it was the day when the worst was suspected and then confirmed. On the night of Day Two I had stayed at home with Harry. Mary Ellen kept in constant contact and told me she rose from the small couch in Louis's hospital room at two o'clock in the morning so that she could accompany our son to the **CT** scan that Dr. Beardsley had ordered. Medical science says that one session of CT (Computerized Tomography) "is worth a roomful of neurologists." It enables doctors and researchers to roam through the body's interior and image anything unexpected. Dr. Diana Beardsley had a mental list of things to look for that she hoped not to find.

I returned to New Haven, and resumed my note-taking by Louis's bedside. Here's a sample of that day:

> *CT scan done at 2 am > no results given at that time. Lou had blood taken from his foot because he has small veins. Frustration with lack of information from all areas. Surgeon to place the line for IV still not sure when. Lou will continue to have blood work done to check cell counts. Meeting with Dr. Beardsley shortly to get up-to-date.*

The CT scan represented one of the easier moments in that first major collection of vital data—an experience that's always more difficult for a pediatric patient than an adult one. I came to learn that taking blood from the foot is not unusual. Police on drug busts think they know where to look for needle traces, but furtive addicts often choose the foot instead of the more visible arm. I didn't like comparing my little boy with an addict, but I was determined to learn everything and anything that might be helpful. So, now I appreciated that a pediatric nurse or a doctor may have to search far and wide for a workable **vein**.

My frustration escalated. My wife and I felt that we weren't getting sufficient information. There seemed to be an unnecessary lack of information sharing. We had seen no sign of progress: Where, for instance, were the bone marrow results? One solid benefit of keeping detailed notes was that I could look back on each day and then list results to look for the next day.

As we stood, sat, and paced in Louis's room we became aware of an ascending list of procedures: blood and urine tests; bone marrow biopsies; intravenous line insertions for chemotherapy and fluids.

Back in 2001, parents or patients who asked for details in hospitals were, by and large, unusual, and hospitals had no habit or tradition of giving out specifics. I realized that every severe and sudden illness produced a dynamic situation, where procedures may be altered or dropped according to the arrival of new information and new opinions. I realized the medical staff was under time constraints and that there many patients' needs that came before mine.

Nevertheless, it's my nature to ask questions and to expect answers. My wife and I probably pressed harder to get the details than most people did back then. As we were not able to get any clear answers from anyone we asked for a new meeting with Dr. Beardsley. After three days of tests surely a diagnosis must be at hand. One thing we did learn from the nurses was that cancer cells reproduce quickly and the sooner treatment starts the better.

Every day, hour, and minute of delay allows the predators inside our son to multiply at will.

All we really knew so far was that leukemia still remained, it seemed, the likely diagnosis. A hospital social worker arrived and reinforced this by handing us leaflets detailing leukemia support groups, parking advice and coupons at the hospital for the long treatment, and visiting days ahead. We remained polite and grateful but our insides were eating us alive.

At two-thirty on Friday afternoon, in a tiny room on the pediatric oncology floor at Yale New Haven Hospital, we met Doctor Beardsley again. Exuding calm and respect, she reported on all of Louis's symptoms, including, as she had thought, some fullness on the left side of his stomach, which possibly suggested a kidney enlargement. Mary Ellen had also noticed some abdominal swelling, but nothing alarming in a small child.

Dr. Beardsley gently revealed the results of the CT scan which showed a "mass," i.e., a tumor above the kidney on the left. Would the towering waves from this tsunami ever stop? Facts had always represented solid ground to me, so I hadn't counted on reacting with this sickening feeling of dread. I felt the ground under my feet give way. I grabbed my note pad for support and started writing.

November 23:

Fullness of left side of stomach – kidney enlarged.

Malignant cells did not type as leukemia but CAT scan shows 6 cm mass/tumor above kidney on left.

*Tumor in the **adrenal gland***

>controls blood pressure > urine will show type of cancer.

***Neuroblastoma** – child tumor – maybe – 8 pm test ready. Postpone placing the line because he will need more marrow taken. May also need biopsy if tumor in widespread advanced stage. Prelim urine result is neuroblastoma > not clear what type.*

Writing these facts helped me absorb the situation and by doing that regain a miniscule degree of control over my child's life. The tumor in the adrenal gland on Louis's left side had **malignant** cells that were wholly unexpected. Dr. Beardsley (who was accompanied by a hospital social worker trained in helping shocked patients and relatives) no longer diagnosed A.L.L. or A.M.L. or any kind of leukemia whatsoever. Her diagnosis was one that we had never heard—Neuroblastoma. The next two words I had heard before, but I had no idea how such familiar words would turn my life upside down—"**Stage four.**"

Initially, my wife and I could only guess what we and Louis faced. We had been knocked off our feet again. While we had Dr. Beardsley's attention there was no room for tears or sorrow, we simply asked the major and most natural question: What are the chances? Dr. Beardsley indicated the standard expectation—no more than twenty-five to thirty per cent survival. Many specialists believed it incurable.

Squeezed around a tiny table in an oppressively cramped room at Yale New Haven Hospital, with a social worker and a nurse standing by, Dr. Beardsley noted a crucial and highly visible detail. She said that Louis had begun to exhibit one of the known external effects of neuroblastoma—dark, raccoon-like circles around his eyes. This, she said, indicated bone involvement at the base of the skull; she was too tactful and kind to add that "raccoon eyes" are the hallmark of an aggressive form of the disease.

Naturally, our impulse was to discuss this new diagnosis with the Dr. we knew best, Dr. Gregory Germain. At this point, he had been a pediatrician in private practice for five or six years and yet this was only his second neuroblastoma case.

"The first one I also remember vividly, and that child had Stage Four neuroblastoma just like Louis—and she died. And she died pretty quickly and aggressively, and I'd like to say I learned a lot from her case that benefitted Louis, and how I handled this. But that memory was stuck in my mind as I sat and talked to you that day," Dr. Germain told us some years later.

We let loose an avalanche of questions, the principle one being: Can it be confirmed? Yes, Dr. Germain told us, a simple urine test would confirm neuroblastoma. Of course we entertained the inkling of a doubt—maybe they got this wrong.

Dr. Germain had told us that "there may be some kind of genetic switch that may get flipped by a constellation of viruses. It's all beyond our understanding."

Mary Ellen considered it "so kind of Dr. Germain to try and relieve some of the anguish that we were feeling." I agreed and felt profound gratitude that we had found a compassionate doctor willing to hear us think this through. We were Louis's parents and our attitude would affect him. We needed to be positive, not self-blaming.

With Doctor Germain's kind help we were able to transition to a more productive set of questions: What do we do next? How do we fix this? What about our other son, Harry? Who can help us?

The race began to find world-class resources. As a self-reliant and resourceful person I dove head-first into Google searches using the terms "pediatric oncologist" and "neuroblastoma." I swam towards many names and worked hard to find a fit. One name jumped out—Dr. Nai-Kong V. Cheung, a graduate of Harvard and MIT, is head of the Neuroblastoma Team at Memorial Sloan-Kettering Hospital in New York. He's a pediatric oncologist who said he had "one simple and single purpose—to cure neuroblastoma."

I learned that of the 350 or so patients diagnosed with Stage Four neuroblastoma in the United States in any one year, Dr. Cheung's unit receives almost a quarter of those classified as high- risk. Many are relapsed, therefore in danger of dying, and referred in the hope that they can be saved. This fact may not be surprising, given Sloan-Kettering's universal reputation as a cancer hospital.

I filed Dr. Cheung's name in my mind along with the Memorial Sloan-Kettering Hospital and got on with the present moment.

Meanwhile, Dr. Beardsley at Yale began to set out a practical plan. First, she said that she probably would not need a biopsy of the tumor (which they would address with chemotherapy), even though the scan told them that it measured six centimeters, a large mass in a small body. Then, to our alarm, Dr. Beardsley said that she wanted a second bone marrow biopsy. We could not imagine why this would be necessary. Dear little Louis had already endured one bone marrow invasion with very little anesthetic on Thanksgiving Day. It soon became evident that the first biopsy tests were lost somewhere in the digital ether. We suppressed our outrage. What good would that do? We did learn that following up quickly on test results was important. The squeaky wheel does get the grease even in the medical world.

Suddenly, a new doctor presented himself: Dr. John Seashore, a pediatric surgeon employed at Yale. Dr. Beardsley asked Dr. Seashore to install in Louis's body the "permanent" intravenous line, a **portacath**, a single line catheter implanted under the skin and connected to a vein.

Mary Ellen and I embarked on an entirely new and unchosen course of education that had a vast vocabulary of its own. Doctors and nurses often have two or three different words for the same procedure, medication, medical device, test, bandage, needle, etc. Learning just one was never enough as doctors frequently interchanged these words. It just made the learning curve a little steeper. Having heard for the first time the words neuroblastoma and **metastasize**, we now heard **superior vena cava** catheter, or SVC. No sooner had we heard this incomprehensible string of syllables than we learned the first line was about to be inserted into our son's body. Naturally, I needed to take notes and here they are:

> *Central Line – Superior Vena Cava catheter insertion portacath – stays below skin - must stick in w/a needle to penetrate – lower risk of infection – put crème onto numb skin.*

The surgeon, in this case Dr. Seashore, had plans to slide a pliable silicone tube into the large vein that goes straight into our little boy's heart. Even at that early stage, Dr. Beardsley's team had already given Mary Ellen the name of an emulsive cream, **Emla**, a topical anesthetic to spread on the skin around the risk-prone insertion point, to help relieve the pain of pushing the needle into the **mediport**; ("Amazing product," Mary Ellen commented to me later, "that our insurance stopped covering mid-treatment.")

Another word we quickly learned was **metabolites**. We learned it because neuroblastoma produces substances that show up in urine and can give useful clues about how well the body is working.

While Dr. Beardsley gave us as much clinical information as we could handle, inadvertently making us experts in medical terminology, she was also drawing us into an awareness of process. In the gentlest possible way we learned that doctors are not magicians and they do not know everything about everything. We learned this one moment at a time as we inched forward on our frightening path, listening as intently as our whirling emotions would allow.

Whenever I felt in danger of falling off the cliff, I pulled out my notebook and began to scribble notes by way of staying in the present moment. Here's another sample:

> *Need to do bone m. & CT headscan & X-rays & MRI. Rarely have neuroblastoma in brain. Tumor started in adrenal gland. Needs to be treated systemically and are reactive to Chemo.*

Continuing her tutoring, Dr. Beardsley gave us further helpful information, clinical and non-clinical. First, she explained to us the word **"protocol"** as it applied to us and to all other parents in this predicament.

Next, Dr. Beardsley introduced us to the existence of COG, the Children's Oncology Group. Any doctor in the field is aware of current COG protocol, and knows where, and how, to find it. The COG protocol is developed by the leading pediatric oncologists from around the world who treat a specific children's cancer. These top doctors all gather and agree on a fixed treatment procedure called a protocol. The goal is to establish a global standard of care that has been scientifically proven through years of applied studies by the largest number of oncologists. The COG protocols are updated on a regular basis.

For oncologists who do not treat a rare cancer, such as neuroblastoma, utilizing the latest COG protocol is the safest and most effective treatment available that has been peer reviewed and approved. Although we did not know it at the time it made perfect sense for Yale to use the COG protocol. We also learned later that the latest breakthrough treatments are normally not included in the COG protocols.

In November 2001, the doctors at Yale New Haven Hospital were working from the COG neuroblastoma playbook.

It was at this point that I asked the most important questions of Louis's life. I had found these during my online research and knew that they had to be asked. They were tough questions and I knew it. Dr. Beardsley handled them with astute professionalism:

1. What was the survival rate on the COG protocol Louis was to follow?
Answer: 30%
2. How many cases of neuroblastoma had Yale treated over the past year?
Answer: 2
3. How many of the kids treated at Yale had survived?
Answer: One was doing well.

After taking in the information, Dr. Beardsley directed us to learn more about neuroblastoma which (large understatement) we did. In the process, we also trained, hour by hour, and not yet consciously, how to become super-advocates for our son, Louis.

With this foundation in place, Dr. Beardsley then began to spell out more details of what we could expect for Louis. Medical terms flew like strange birds around our heads. I captured them in my notes, for example:

> **Stem cell** transplants w/high dose chemotherapy. Can have Lou's own stem cells removed after chemo. They filter out stem cells & freeze them to put back later after chemo. **Biological markers** are important to determine the type of NB. Favorable markers vs. unfavorable - less likely to be unfavorable. We requested second opinion.

It was a very steep learning curve that felt precarious every step of the way. Mary Ellen remembers it this way, "I honestly didn't know what chemotherapy was, other than treatment for cancer." We could both grasp the basic concept of a "high-dose chemotherapy"—but what regular parent knows the workings of a stem cell transplant, biological markers, or a **bone marrow transplant**?

It was necessary to understand all these words and procedures though it was like learning a new language. My methodology was as follows: grasp the word from the doctor's mouth, connect it to a tangible procedure Louis had to undertake, and write it down. This is often called "immersion learning." I would ask a lot of questions along the way and then be able to connect the dots. Developing an appreciation for the intricate steps involved allowed me to develop genuine awe at their expertise and to mix this with increased knowledge and patience of my own.

Day three of the nightmare included many of the most intense meetings of my life. It was relentless. There was no down time. It was the proverbial fire hose like I had never experienced in my life. Every second mattered.

Dr. Beardsley pressed on demonstrating impressive stamina. With not enough clinical information or test results to nail everything down, she began to outline the treatment that would likely follow, and some of its effects. Lou could expect: transfusions to bring up his cell counts; ongoing scans; and biopsies to determine the challenges as precisely as possible. And whatever the biological markers, there would of course be chemotherapy, administered in the hospital for three to four days in succession followed by out-patient treatments as needed. I took to my note pad to stop my own head from spinning:

> *Purged bone marrow > 6 courses of Chemo - A course of chemo 3/4 days in hospital - low blood counts – 21 days apart – the next chemo 9/15 days later. Modern prevention medication. Sterility likely. Possible hearing loss – high frequency – Constipation. 150 days of treatment approx. at first. No exposure to sick people. 150 days of follow-up treatment. Lots of info coming at us at once. Allopurinol to prevent **crystallization** of urine*

The hospital had been having mixed success in its data-gathering so far and had made some mistakes. As with the missing bone marrow biopsy, Louis's early bloodwork for biological markers, sent by Yale to Minnesota, also vanished, and had to be re-done. The markers were important as to the aggressiveness of the cancer and the likelihood of survival. Surprisingly, the treatment protocol would not be impacted by the marker results, so there were no delays due to this error. However, Louis did have to repeat the bone marrow biopsy due to the hospital error. We both did not understand how this could happen in such a famous hospital. Losing a document is one thing but a set of biopsies from our son was at a whole different level. We did our best to handle this news because there was nothing we could do about it except wonder what may go wrong next.

My frustration threshold was starting to crack. Mary Ellen and I could not see things happening with a sense of urgency. We refrained from screaming all the following questions: When will treatment begin? When will you know enough to get the chemotherapy started? It's been too many days—the cancer's spreading fast—every minute! Shouldn't something be happening soon? Right now, in fact?

We did get some relief. As the medical team awaited the results of some tests, and prepared the small patient for new investigations, they began to release details a little more freely. They explained procedures and they even admitted to the reasons for the delay. And insofar as our feelings could ever improve in such appalling circumstances, Mary Ellen and I felt a degree better.

Despite our understandable bewilderment, we had grasped an essential fact—we needed to settle down and get a grip on the size of what we faced along with all the attendant possibilities, good and bad. We had to learn to live in a grey area. We wanted to be informed in great detail if possible. I called it "maintenance" information. I have never liked surprises, especially bad ones. I need time to accept a fact I don't like and that I can't change. So I kept asking for the schedule of treatments.

I was privately distressed when learning about the probable and irreversible personal costs to unsuspecting little Louis: constipation in the short term; partial deafness forever; hair loss; mouth sores; low blood counts; a severely compromised immune system; likely shortness of physical stature; life-threatening danger of liver infections; heart damage; secondary cancers, sterility; etc. The list of side-effects and potential short-and long-term likely problems was mind-boggling. A normal person would never agree to these treatments unless the alternative was even worse.

Mary Ellen remained at Louis's side at all times to watch over him and tend to his needs. She protected him, fed him, changed him, read to him, and made sure our three-year-old boy was loved at all times. I would sit by his bed for hours doing research online, reading, and writing notes. We were both riding the learning curve as best as we could.

The hospital postponed placing the portacath until the second bone marrow biopsy took place— which happened at eight o'clock on the evening of the third day, Friday, 23 November. This time, Louis had some sedation—he called it "tiger milk," a drug named **Propofol**. Fortunately, it sedated Louis for the entire procedure so he suffered no pain. This was a blessing as no three year-old should suffer pain when it can be avoided.

When he had to have his "tiger milk," Mary Ellen and I only stayed with him until it made him unconscious and peaceful. Watching him gradually fall unconscious would bring tears every time.

By now, that common marker of neuroblastoma was becoming more and more visible: Louis clearly had the raccoon blackness around his eyes. And thus, any remote, lingering hope that he hadn't been attacked by this monster, this neuroblastoma, truly began to fade.

And yet, on that November evening, as I was at home tucking in our older child, and Mary Ellen sat watchful beside our younger son in the Children's Hospital at Yale, a unit attached to one of the most renowned medical schools in the world, we both deliberately chose hope over despair.

With lives already full and busy, and no previous experience of anything like this, and little or no knowledge regarding medicine or its depths, we had launched ourselves into an effort almost beyond our imagination in its intensity. Working against the tight, respected and stern conventions of hospital practices, we were constructing an instinctive, strenuous and forceful parental effort at **advocacy**. Here, at the beginning of the crisis, we acted like a pair of warriors, edging forward, side by side, over desperate terrain, watching out for one another as we peered ahead, not knowing the rage of this lethal creature coming toward us to devour our child. My wife and I were 100% in tune with each other, knowing we would fight this beast as we had never fought anything.

CHAPTER 4: DAY FOUR

Here are some of my notes from day four:

> *Saturday, November 24:*
> *Lou goes into surgery at 8 am to place central IV line &*
> *to get further marrow samples for marking of the*
> *neuroblastoma> Out of surgery at 9.30> All went well>*
> *10.30 goes into full body CT scan to get base line on his*
> *organs and before chemo > His **CBC** counts are improved*
> *but still low **Hemoglobin** 9 vs 11 normal> Harry and I*
> *spend the morning together – Harry is very concerned that*
> *he is not getting enough attention> So Harry and I napped*
> *together and painted his car together> Harry also wants to*
> *spend time w/ his mom.*

My wife and I were beginning to worry about Harry, who is two years older than Louis. The boys were always very close and played together constantly. We lived in a modern house in the middle of the woods where the brothers could roam freely to explore nature's gifts. They loved to explore together and often came back carrying such gifts as: frogs, snakes, mushrooms, and leaves. They loved each other and even slept in the same room together.

Now, Harry had been ripped away from his brother and best friend. His parents were consumed with his brother in a strange place called a hospital. While Harry was also worried about Louis, he was sad that life was not normal. Mommy was devoting more time to Lou than him, and from his point-of- view that was just not fair. Harry could not understand what was happening and we struggled to explain it to him at first. We tried to reassure him that all was going to be ok, that Louis was very sick, and we had to take care of him now.

Harry could read our emotions well and knew that he had to be a good boy. He just wanted to be loved like his brother and get his share of time with mommy and daddy. We tried hard to give Harry attention but it was often impossible. Our youngest son needed all we could muster.

And still Lou was under attack from the cancer spreading like prairie fire in his system and, moment by moment, the malignant cells multiplied. Twelve hours later, next morning, Louis entered surgery again, for the implantation of a central intravenous line—another physical invasion. Two hours after that, he lay down and was drawn through the space-age machine of the full body CT scan, where he was instructed not to move for thirty minutes. He wasn't yet four years old.

As if he had the training of a Yale Drama School graduate student, Louis began performing the role of a model patient. It seemed incredible. He worked out his own attitude towards the doctors and nurses, he stayed just on the right side (according to all the reports) of impertinence; he teased them, he responded to them, made mock biting attacks on them with his T-rex toy, and he told a few of them that if they hurt him, his dinosaur would bite them. He bantered and improvised like a professional. He made hardcore medical staff deeply care about him and comment on his courage. Without fuss or tantrum he did precisely what they needed him to do. Louis remembers his attitude this way: "Let's get this over with now so I can go back to playing. There were a few painful moments certainly, like one time they couldn't get a needle into my vein, so they had to stick me nine times to try to get it. But the thing is, I used to have this hand dinosaur puppet, and so I told the doctors that if you hurt me, I'll let him bite you."

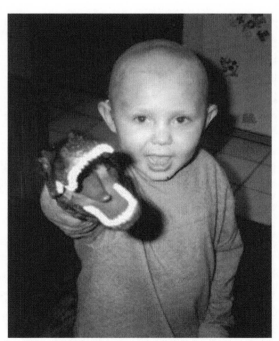

Lou's favorite Dinosaur hand puppet – Doctors beware!

27

Imagine constructing this attitude and delivering this level of cooperation after going several crushing rounds in a ring where you might lose your life!

This merry and obedient behavior worried me slightly. How long could such a winning child, cheerful and loving, maintain this upbeat behavior given such a dire situation? Childhood is supposed to be a magical, protected time that allows for the gentle development of personality, interests, friendships, and intellect. His capacity to deal with pain, and his sophisticated relationships with the doctors and nurses who were sticking needles into him indicated an extraordinary physical and spiritual strength. Were he fortunate enough to survive, it seemed he could achieve the impossible. I was doing everything in my power to make sure his future would be happening.

How do you parent a child in such circumstances? What do you do about the other child in the family? Who, no matter how much he wants to help in sharing the family anguish, is too young to know what's going on, and can't but feel that his younger brother is getting all the attention. Of course Lou was getting all the attention. That was unavoidable and appropriate. I cautioned myself against living in the future.

At the end of that first half-week, the comparative ease that is America's Saturday brought a kind of respite—dangerous in a way because that's when people know how strung out they are. While monitoring everything that was going on around Louis—the IV procedures, the scans, the blood counts—Mary Ellen and I took some time out and went to an Indian restaurant for dinner, our first time alone as a couple since Wednesday morning, our first time to step aside with any breathing space—and therefore our first time to let the twin blankets of hope and despair settle over us. My new habit of being a note-taking observer allowed me to see the exhausting toll that Mary Ellen's minute-by-minute parenting in the hospital had been taking. Later that night I noted:

> *Mel is getting tired and overloaded. Not enough sleep, too much worry & exhaustion are setting in. She needs a break. Mel and I went to Indian Palace for dinner – nice break, but our hearts are heavy.*

After dinner, she went back to Louis's bedside, and I went home to take care of Harry, and keep the house and our altered domestic life in some type of order. A new pattern had been forged for the Unger family. Some relief lay in the fact that I could begin to see ahead and assess what the next phase of our new life would look like. It was now eighty hours since we had driven to the pediatrician, and then to the Emergency Room at Yale New Haven Hospital. It was as though an accident had occurred— a force had hit us out of the blue.

CHAPTER 5: DAY FIVE

The next day, Sunday, November 25, day five, became the busiest so far. Taking notes kept me alert and present. I tried to focus on what was to happen immediately, and why; what had to be prepared for, and why; and then list the possible outcomes and next steps—and why. These notes gave me something to hold onto literally and figuratively.

> *Lou went into **MRI** this morning – he was put under full anesthesia. Has extended abdomen & pees a lot – maybe fluid pushing on bladder. Test schedule for Nov. 26 01: 9 am – Skeletal Survey – bones X-ray: 11am*
> *– bone scan – w/ dye - no dye? 3 pm bone scan w/dye Chemo > vesicants*
> *– needs to lie down. Meet w/ Dr. Beardsley 11:15 am – Harvesting stem cells would need second line after 2nd round. Has urinary urgency –*
> *peeing more frequently. Today red blood cells 23.8*
> *– 36 normal – 15 when he came in: 12 hemoglobin – 5 when he came in: Cancer in bone marrow takes over the space.*
> *– Course of treatment is per the Children's Oncology Group: Dr. Diller at Dana-Farber to review – for 2nd opinion - suggested by Dr. Beardsley*

Be careful what you wish for: the flow of medical and treatment details became a flood, then a torrent. Although the words were on the paper in front of me I could only comprehend the ones I already knew. There was always so much new information to digest and doctors do not make it easy on parents.

In the 11:15 morning meeting, Dr. Beardsley gave us a graduate-level lecture on chemotherapy.

First, she outlined the procedures, and named the investigations planned, principally a skeletal scan with dye to highlight where cancer might have attacked the bones. Then she reported on any changes observed; principally that the transfusions were helping; the oxygen-carrying, red blood cell count was climbing back up in the direction of normal— improved by 50% since Louis was admitted to Yale New Haven

Hospital but one third short of the ideal 36 (the measurement derives from the percentage level of cells deemed necessary in a liter of blood).

In response to my request for a second opinion on the diagnosis and the prognosis, Dr. Beardsley referred me to Dr. Lisa Diller, a pediatric oncologist at the Dana-Farber Cancer institute in Boston. (She would in due course confirm every word of Dr. Beardsley's diagnosis and treatment.)

Another new word cropped up in conversation with Dr. Beardsley: **ganglioneuroblastoma**. In my son's case it meant that the tumor arising from his adrenal gland had indeed formed from a bundling of nerve cells. My response was to fight back with notes. Somehow, if I could keep pace with all of this, surely we would gain some ground, went my unconscious thinking. I was also afraid of forgetting an important detail.

> *Will give us a calendar of chemo 6 X chemo – 4 are the same Chemo. 2 same types > 1 different > Harvest 1 same type > Harvest. Different after cancer is out of marrow > Tumor reduction & ganglioneurosis – get the tumor > Then may need transplant of stem cells to get marrow back. Radiation treatment at end. Possible antibody. Pediatric Oncology Heart function > extra muscle due to anemia. Chamber enlarged but will likely go back to normal once anemia is gone. 1st cycle of chemo > will need transfusions of red blood cells and platelets.*

I would advise parents who are advocating for their child to keep good notes and keep asking questions. Advocating for a patient is more common now than when we went through this, nevertheless, I know it's a human response to crumble in the face of traumatic medical news. Hang in there. Inform yourself. Become a knowledgeable advocate and keep asking questions. The best doctors love questions and appreciate informed parents. Our team eventually allowed information to flow freely, but it was a gradual process.

Dr. Beardsley described the stages of treatment—two different types of chemotherapy would be delivered to Louis. The primary objective would be to attack the tumor along with the remaining neuroblastoma cells. Since this would also destroy his bone marrow, the second stage would be to renew the bone marrow, to re-grow it, through a transplant of healthy stem cells. In hindsight, my notes were not always accurate, but our understanding grew with repetition and continual questions. In this way, somehow, knowledge was constantly transferred.

It was agonizing to sit through long meetings such as this. I desperately wanted to be with Louis and comfort him, as did my wife. However, Louis was remarkably undemanding. He was content to watch television and color Bob the Builder books.

In this meeting, Dr. Beardsley also outlined two other possible treatments—radiation and antibody treatment. Before that could happen, Louis's overall health had to be under control, his red cell counts being especially important.

Dr. Beardsley kept encouraging Mary Ellen and I to look not just ahead but around. Moment by moment, I had one basic response and that was to acquire and own as much information as I could, believing I could help.

> *Need to have special diet. Mouth care important.* **Relapses** *are biggest enemy. May have some* **radiation** *treatment if brain and spinal are affected. 4 X Chemo start tomorrow*
>
> *> Drugs* **Vincristine** *drug – Hair loss, constipation - can burn the skin if not properly inserted red urine/pink can affect heart function - 300mg total – if you get more than 600mg in a life can have heart problems >* **Doxorubicin** *> same Adriamycin >* **Cyclophosphamide** *goes out through kidneys & can cause bladder damage Sterility> After 24 hours of chemo – start shots for rejuvenation 2 X Chemo – 3rd type* **Cisplatin** *- causes vomiting, can affect kidneys one hour after taking - affect his frequency hearing* **Etoposide** *(UP16) – may cause secondary tumors later*

At this point, Dr. Beardsley identified the two principal drugs that would be powered into Louis—Vincristine and Doxorubicin, plus a third: Cisplatin.

When asked if we had any questions, Mary Ellen and I pressed for knowledge about side effects

Doxorubicin, a synthetic drug also called **Adriamycin**, aims at the bone marrow, and can cause nausea, mouth sores, loss of appetite, stomach pain, diarrhea, and heart damage— in short, many of the symptoms associated with most high-dose chemotherapy.

Cisplatin, also a cancer destroyer, has a platinum base, and may cause loss of hearing.

It was too much to take in, but we listened to the answer along with a description of some general risks assumed with chemotherapy drugs. Louis would be running the risk of kidney and heart problems, depending on the dosage that he would eventually receive. I knew that he already had some heart enlargement due to the pervasiveness and severity of his cancer (if there's anemia, the heart has to pump faster to get oxygen to the brain) although that could likely return to normal in the event of a cure. In addition to the piling on of chemotherapy drugs, Louis would continue to need transfusions to keep up his platelets count, attacked by the chemo— because the neuroblastoma was still attacking him. In the pauses, Mary Ellen and I would look each other in the eyes and see our own fear staring back.

And while receiving all this information and horror I was silently screaming: "No treatment yet! Stop the cancer now! I am getting really pissed off!"

Dr. Beardsley mentioned a fourth anti-cancer drug that might be included, depending on progress or the lack of it—**Etoposide**. Derived from the mandrake plant, usually known as the mayapple, and indigenous to North America, Etoposide causes, among other things, loss of hair, also caused by other drugs. Indeed they all came with side effects ranging from the unpleasant to the dangerous: that's chemotherapy— and none of it comprehensible to a three-year-old child. How do we prepare Louis for all this?

Buried in my notes, was a passing remark that would come back to haunt us: *Relapses are biggest enemy.* I had no idea that most doctors believed relapses to be universally fatal. This fact had seemed remote and did not strike me as needing elaboration at that moment. I had to deal with the current reality. I wanted to make sure that, as a first measure, my wife and I understood the chemotherapy procedure as fully as possible. And anyway, I agreed with Mary Ellen when she said, "What-ifs will kill you. You have to focus on the task at hand."

In this newly vigorous information stream, the Yale team gave us a leaflet by the Center for Cancer and Blood disorders at the Children's Hospital at Richland Memorial Hospital in Columbia, South Carolina. I immediately began reading the questions most frequently asked by bewildered parents (FAQs).

On the first page it said: "There is no answer [as] to the cause of neuroblastoma at this time. We do know that it is NOT contagious. We also know that some infants are born with it, suggesting that it can occur while the unborn child's nervous system cells are growing and maturing. In this case the cells remain immature and develop into neuroblastoma." This information was simultaneously alarming and reassuring.

I quickly learned that it does NOT tend to run in families or occur in multiple family members. That was good to know. However, my spirit took another hit when I read that neuroblastoma spreads very easily, most commonly in the belly or to the bones and the skin. I didn't know the word **Metastases** and made a note to look that up.

There was a detailed account of "Staging"— the rising levels of the disease, Stages One through Four. The leaflet also described CAT scans, bone scans, and ultrasound in simple terms. It also explained the reasons for urine collections, blood tests, and biopsies. The page headed How Can Neuroblastoma Be Treated? outlined three of the typical possibilities: surgery, radiation, and chemotherapy. The efficacy according to the patient's age is discussed. At that point I had truly reached overload, but kept going with the hope of learning some kind of magic that would end the nightmare.

The pamphlet included a topic not often addressed by doctors—the emotions. Under the question, Are My Feelings Normal and What Can I do About Them? came the following answer: "It is shocking and overwhelming to hear that your child has cancer. Initially you may not believe it, or hope that the diagnosis is wrong. However, the changes you see in your child and the experience of being in the hospital and beginning treatment will confirm the reality of your situation. Many family members will often feel that they are somehow responsible for the child's disease, or feel guilty that they were not able to detect it sooner. Remember that this disease does not usually become noticeable until it is quite advanced. It is a "silent tumor" in its early stages. It cannot be caused or triggered by anything anyone could do to or feed the child (this includes during pregnancy with the child)."

It was strangely comforting to visualize Louis as an outpatient, being driven on treatment days into New Haven by his mom, who would sit in a chair on the second floor of the Children's Hospital at Yale, like so many other parents, while our child intravenously received his transfusions alongside other small patients.

Meanwhile, Louis was making over his hospital room with toys, drawings, books, and stuffed animals. He was permanently attached to an

IV pole and had become an expert at riding it down the hallway like he was on a medical skateboard. The blood transfusions had revived his energy like we hadn't seen it in weeks and he was making the best of his situation. He often wanted to go to the playroom, where they had all types of toys, drawing materials, and books for him to explore. With his outwardly improving strength and attitude we were also feeling optimistic. Louis never let neuroblastoma get in his way of having fun. His brother was always by his side whenever possible.

That Sunday night, we had relatives from both sides of the family visit Louis in the hospital.

Naturally, we did our best to prepare them for what they would see. It did us all so much good to cheer each other up. It was very hard for our relatives to deal with Louis at first. Clearly afraid of hurting him they gently kissed and hugged him at the same time. Lou rose to the occasion, happy to be at the center of such loving attention.

Later that night, at home again, I found myself initiating a very unexpected activity. I had the impulse to write about our situation to friends, family, and our company employees across the globe.

Eventually, I would send several hundred e-mails to people, lay and medical, whom I had never met or been referred to, and whom I would never meet.

Finding the words for such news was extremely difficult. Nevertheless, I began by writing what I thought of as "Louis's Battle Log" and I wrote from Louis's point of view. It simply made sense to write with his voice and perspective. I needed to tell people what was happening. I had gone missing at work since Thanksgiving, had appeared erratically, and had given no explanations. I could not find my own words to describe the situation. However, with the help of Louis's spirit, the words began to flow. After hitting send, I sobbed uncontrollably for the first time since we saw Dr. Germain. The weight and reality of our situation hit me hard and it was a relief to let go.

With the subject line, "My 3-year-old son is diagnosed with cancer," I sent the very first e-mail to friends and family;

Nov 25, 2001

Hi everybody.

My name is Lou and I am in a comfy hospital bed right

now watching my favorite Bob the Builder video. On Wednesday I went to see the doctor and I haven't been home since. I have to stay in a hospital for a while to get medicine. They put me in big noisy machines all the time. Mommy goes with me so I am not so scared.

Strange people have been sticking me with needles and I don't like that. I always have a plastic tube connected to me now. My Mommy and Daddy told me that I need to be strong and brave so I can be better soon. All the nurses are really nice and give me chocolate milk whenever I want some. They call me "Big Lou" because I am so brave.

My big brother Harry likes to play with me even though I am sick. I like it when Glenn and my friends come to play with me too. I really like it when I get toys to play with. I want to go home soon.

Mommy and Daddy told me I will get a lot of medicine soon that can make me tired, and my tummy hurt. I have to be very strong and brave for a long time to get better. I know I can do it. I hope everyone comes and plays with me because I like to play. I get to see my Daddy a lot now. He said he is going to take care of all of us until I get better.

I want to play with my new game, but Daddy says I have to go to sleep now. He sleeps on the couch in my room.

Nite Nite—I love you to the moon and back.

Lou

CHAPTER 6: DAY SIX

Day six was Monday, November 26. I woke up to clear blue skies over New Haven and a mild and unseasonal 62° temperature outside. Looking out the window gave me a glimpse of the world I used to know. Rather than develop any negative thoughts, I began note-taking for the day.

> *Tough night for me w/ Lou > I wrote e-mails to everyone in the company & separate ones to managers. Grief set in. Lou got up at 11.00 to pee on me, floor, banister. Took blood sample at 6 am & we were up.*
>
> *I feel tired & exhausted. Lou was supposed to get X-ray this am at 9 am – skeletal survey 11 am bone scan – no dye. 3 pm bone scan – w/ dye.*
>
> *Received dye in tracer at 1 pm needs only 2 hrs to go through. Bone scan will take ¾ - 1 hr.*

So by this sixth day of the crisis there had been no actual remedial action. There had simply been countless tests and blood transfusions. The medical team at Yale had posted the impending treatment, though, and I made notes from their notes about what would be happening soon. I needed to remain patient and positive. So, I made notes and Googled words that were new to me.

> *1st chemo – Vincristine & Doxorubicin over 72 hours continuous- main line.*

> ***Cyclophosphamide*** *6 hrs infusion &*
> ***Mesna*** *pulses every 3-6 hrs.*

Cyclophosphamide, though efficacious by repute, is also a beast, a problem in itself, and as such it forms part of chemotherapy's frightening lore. With no help from other drugs, it does the infamous damage of chemo—to bone marrow and bones, to hair. It can provoke nausea and stomach pains, and it even introduces other forms of cancer, such as leukemia or **lymphomas**. Everyone using it knows that it's a scorched-earth remedy. Using it begs the question, "Will the fire brigade do more damage than the fire?"

To counter some of the impact, Louis would receive another drug, Mesna, developed as an antidote to the potential rampages of Cyclophosphamide. Mesna is a sodium-aware antioxidant that offers some bladder protection. Taken all in all, chemotherapy is a contradiction in terms: a ferocious healing.

Before starting Louis Unger's chemotherapy, Yale New Haven Hospital's doctors still wanted, still needed, and still sought more data. Mary Ellen and I urgently wanted the curing to start. Our daily meeting with Dr. Beardsley kept us in the loop, and in a mixed report she now had some good news for us. After asking why he needed endless scans and tests and after asking when exactly treatment would begin, Dr. Beardsley gave us some very important information, in simple terms. "We must begin with a baseline evaluation of Louis to know exactly where and how severely the cancer has spread. After every round of chemotherapy we will repeat the same scans and tests to identify any changes. The goal, after all the treatment, is to have the tests show him to be cancer- free." I actually understood what she said immediately and realized how valuable the initial test results would become. We could only know if he was improving by comparing the before and after results—we were in the before stage. Still, my wife and I were burning inside for the treatment to start.

She went on to tell us that the cancer had not shown up in Lou's brain or spinal cord. It had, however, appeared to a small degree in the Lou's eye sockets and arms, and was significant in his legs and lower spine. Of course, that was very, very hard to hear. Mary Ellen and I sat dazed.

Dr. Beardsley continued and we then learned in more detail how the chemotherapy treatment would work. Naturally, I took notes by way of keeping my head on straight.

> *Three drugs go for 2 days – must pee every 2 hours. 2 drugs go for one day – also getting Mesna. 4th day 72 hours of straight chemo.14-21 days counts come up. 2 course of therapy*

> *– He needs second line. Purging of neuroblastoma. Gets anti-nausea meds & 3 additional drugs for nausea & get surgeons to check. Benadryl. Bones hurt > Using newest protocol*

> *> previously: Pediatric Oncology Group Protocol >–*

new Children Oncology Protocol 3973

> *110 cases of child cancer – no more than 5 cases/year. Pilot results of new protocol.*

> *Yale has no chemo Pharmacist on staff 24 hours. She will be in at 7:30 am. Chemo open at 8am – she [Dr. Beardsley] will check personally. Get Chemo exact – ok to start tomorrow*

With assurances of treatment now imminent, and hearing of new drugs being lined up, such as the antihistamine, **Benadryl**, Mary Ellen and I adapted to our new normal. Mary Ellen settled down to the long, practical, maternal haul. She believed we had two jobs. One: give Louis the best and most effective treatment and support care. Two: make sure the bubble of childhood always surrounded him. I love my wife for so many reasons and the fact that she made sure Louis had the chance to continue being a three-year-old, a time of life when a child needs to play, is just one of those reasons.

Mary Ellen's calendar became a medical record, playbook and game plan. Each day's space had enough room for her to enter every chemical that, in front of her eyes, hour by hour, day by day, would go into Louis. She noted treatment after treatment, and the numbered days on that calendar helped her navigate the present and the future. Having the facts about blood counts, platelets, hemoglobin levels, and in due course a timetable of the chemotherapy sessions made her see that time was passing and there would be a resolution. "I needed to lay out treatments in my calendar so that I could name an end date, a goal," she told me.

Mary Ellen's experience had tremendous overlap with my own, but it was also uniquely her own. She almost lived in the hospital. She would dash home to shower, change clothes, and come right back to the hospital. She was also experiencing a different reality from the one I navigated at the hospital. It's fair to say there is a rampant, hidden sexism in the medical world, and within it a whole world of gate- keepers. Many doctors, she found, did not speak to mothers. The secretaries and assistants to doctors, she observed, "didn't take mothers seriously, didn't give as much weight to the mother's concerns." She would make a call, be put on hold for twenty minutes and then sometimes be transferred to an intern or some medical student. The fact that mothers are most often the primary care-givers didn't resonate with doctors. Mary Ellen discovered early that if she needed information her best chance of acquiring it quickly was through me. If I called, I got an immediate answer. In the interest of helping Louis, she realized this, and as she puts it, simply swallowed her anger, frustration, and disbelief. We operated as a unit and did what we had to do to help Louis and Harry.

"This didn't take much doing. When I found out how it was - it didn't matter. Putting aside my outrage was no big deal. I would have done anything to save Louis," Mary Ellen said later. And at both hospitals she found a responsive group of professionals: on-the-ground nurses.

CHAPTER 7: DAY SEVEN

Day seven was Tuesday, November 27, 2001. At last the healing began. At noon, the fierce Cyclophosphamide was administered. And now that the treatment was under way the hospital staff begin to prepare Mary Ellen and me for the next phase—the care that Louis would need when he went home in a few days. We were expected to learn an awful lot in a short space of time. My note-taking became vital, possibly a matter of life and death.

> *When at Home – counts will drop - little red specks on chest or arms means platelet count is low. Pale, bruising, tired, means counts are dropping- if he has fever, not feeling well call Dr. Beardsley ASAP - 7-10 days counts will drop from start of chemo*
> *6-7 hours from start of chemo – nausea will set in – during chemo > [nausea meds always].*
> ***Zofran** – anti-nausea – every 4 hours & 2 doses 2 - Benadryl anti-nausea – every 6 hrs as needed*
> ***Ativan** – every 12 hrs if needed – narcotic*
> ***Mesna** – bladder clearing infused with chemo*
> ***GCSF** injections must be given after chemo – one shot ?? 1/day per day for 7-10 days 2*
> ***Decadron** > every 12 hrs for anti-nausea as needed every 6 hrs Emla crème – lidocaine – for 1 hrs to reduce pain of injection.*

Hospitals provide some education for patients and their relatives. Nevertheless, it is extraordinarily challenging and frightening. A chemotherapy patient in the house creates strenuous demands. Nothing sanitary is achieved by doing something once from now on. Bedding, towels, underwear—everything must be washed rigorously twice on each occasion.

Every toilet, no matter what the usage, must be flushed twice. Ideally, the patient should use toilet facilities that nobody else uses, but if a small child is being assisted in the bathroom, any unavoidable splashes will mean that the area must be scrubbed, and the care-giver must shower.

Soap becomes as vital as food. Those giving the care have to wear gloves when working intimately with the child, then destroy the gloves and wash their hands at least twice with known and effective disinfectant. Why the fierce rigorousness? Because infection is the new enemy at the gate, and everything in the house must be geared towards keeping the enemy out.

No detail was insignificant. Making the effective rinse for mouth care involved boiling water, adding salt, brushing the gums as well as the teeth, for example. As if the physical care-giving weren't enough, the parents would also have to keep watch 24/7 for: fever; bleeding of any kind; any red skin near the intravenous tube entry point, which had to be preserved when idle but kept immaculate for the next chemo round; any sign of gagging, or throwing up pills; any hint of dizziness; and the slightest elevation of heart rate.

In fact, we were told to treat anything that looked a touch, a hint out of the ordinary with as much suspicion as though it were a major and threatening side-effect. Those were the demands made before Louis even had his first chemotherapy. And as a child patient, Louis must also be kept away from children (except Harry), and away from sick adults.

Phase by phase, we also learned how to watch day and night for platelet counts dropping. We scrutinized Louis for those little red specks that I had noted when Dr. Beardsley first mentioned them (known as petechiae, small broken blood cells). We watched for any new pallor, exceptional tiredness, fresh skin bruises, and the onset of a fever however mild. We also learned how to apply the ointments that would prevent any skin burning if treatments had accidentally leaked onto the skin. Already aware of Benadryl, Mesna, and Emla, I noted three more proprietary names—Zofran, **Ativan** and Decadron. A house where somebody is recovering from chemotherapy is a watchtower.

Once the chemotherapy began on that Tuesday at noon, the medical team pumped it into Louis for 72 hours continuously. For a lay person the procedure is a maze. Some chemicals have two or three names, scientific, organic, proprietary, and because the internal effects cannot be viewed, the logic goes to watching for side effects.

In the early 1980s, oncologists noticed that children could rebound from chemotherapy faster than adults. Their bodies were metabolizing and growing faster. Before this realization, kids were given lower dosages than adults as it only made sense to give a child less of a toxic medication than an adult. But survival rates for Leukemia and other cancers in children did not improve so experiments were made with higher dosages, which started to improve outcomes. As doctors started to see the cause and effect of the inverse dosing logic, they began to increase dosages of chemotherapy two to three times that of adults and this led to even better survival statistics. This was a major breakthrough in improving pediatric cancer treatment and without knowing it Louis was to receive dosages of chemo that would have killed a normal adult.

Whoever invented chemo is a rock star. In front of our eyes Louis was absorbing exactly what he needed through the tubes entering his body. With treatment at last underway, everything quietened down. High drama no longer dominated. The game had changed, and so far for the better. Mary Ellen and I tracked the drugs pumping into Louis, and we felt we were finally starting to cure our boy.

> *Chemo continued – threw up every 2 hrs – did not receive more antinausea meds > Great from 10 am – 3pm then weakened. Almost fell asleep at 6 pm. No food or drink. At 8:30 full power – flying like a plane down the hall. Ate grilled cheese.*

CHAPTER 8: DAY EIGHT

On Wednesday, the second day of chemotherapy, I made a sharp observation and had to advocate for Louis more fiercely. Here's how it began:

6 pm Nov 28th:
Dr. Beardsley came in to look at his central line. Slight bleeding on outside. Louis is trying to itch the needle & rubs; it – may cause bleeding at skin level. Concern that caustic chemicals in meds – Vincristine & Doxorubicin (orange) - will leak onto skin. Lou not complaining of any pain. Med. staff came by at 7.30 from Seashore Surgeon team - I wanted to change dressing. Did not even look at meds going. Sara – nurse – told them about meds & they decided to stop & ask Dr. Seashore & Beardsley tomorrow. 9 pm Lou eating grilled cheese – feeling fine – sleep 10:20.

Dr. Beardsley's inspection apparently yielded nothing that she hadn't seen before. It is, however, a miracle that a three-year-old boy can keep in an IV line. On account of the slight bleeding on the outside of the insertion point, I wanted the dressing around the IV port entry changed. We had been instructed that this must be kept meticulously clean. I made some polite noises about this. When the surgical team not only didn't respond, and didn't even inspect the chemo medicines that were running, I felt we were not doing right by Louis and nothing could make me more infuriated than that.

My words became more direct and louder. It was clear that I was not going to let this go. As a direct result, the chemotherapy nurse got the doctors' attention, and she talked to them about my concern that the chemo treatments with their caustic effects might leak and burn Lou's skin. It didn't matter that Louis hadn't complained of any stinging. He had a very high pain threshold and we shouldn't be waiting until a patient is in agony before intervening. The doctors agreed to attend to it next day, and that's how I learned that aggressive patient advocacy works. Almost as a reward, Lou's second day of chemotherapy ended well with a grilled cheese sandwich and sleep for us all.

Learning to stand up for oneself, learning to complain on one's own behalf, even when justified in depth, is one of life's most needed and most difficult skills. It requires emotional and verbal competence. Even confident people don't always do it well, especially if they have been living in a perpetual state of high anxiety and stress. Making myself heard has never been a problem, but I had to find a whole new set of skills when it came to standing up for Louis who couldn't speak for himself.

There is a feeling of deference, even submissiveness towards a doctor or nurse when they speak to you. This is their realm; they have studied for years, passed exams, specialized and honed their skills. Who am I to ask them questions? What is my right to question their decisions and actions? I was always in awe of doctors. They could rattle off every bone in your body in Latin, describe the history and latest treatments for almost any disease known to man, cut you open and repair your organs and save your life. They are incredibly gifted people and we were fortunate that Louis got treated by the best in the world. My deference and humility were appropriate.

We knew that without these gifted doctors and nurses Lou would have no chance of survival—none! Yet, something strange happened, especially after we became semi-permanent residents of the medical world. It became clear that the gods in white coats were in fact human. They made mistakes, had bad days, mixed up prescriptions, were preoccupied, could miss something, had bosses, and were just like the rest of us. We started to realize that they wanted to help Louis and were passionate about their work, but the responsibility for Louis fell squarely on our shoulders. He was a three year-old boy who needed us to manage his medical care and needs constantly. It was our duty to be vigilant and to speak up on his behalf—respectfully and forcefully if necessary—to make sure he was getting the very best of the medical professionals 24/7 for as long as it took. I understand this practice is called Patient Advocacy and it would save Louis's life.

All Tuesday and Wednesday the chemotherapy poured into Louis. We sat close by, talking to him constantly. On Thursday, the eighth day, I made this note:

Nov. 29th:
*Woke up at 8:00 good night's rest IV in arm disconnected & blood flowing out: stopped: new sheets & waking up **afebrile** > "no fever" term – 100.5 is fever - if*

*he has fever he has to go to hospital for 2 days **nadir***

Afebrile means "fever being absent," and "nadir," which usually indicates the lowest point of the starry heavens, here means the moment in chemotherapy when the red and white blood cell counts drop to their lowest. Mary Ellen and I never wanted to learn these words, but we dutifully absorbed them, adding them to the list of things to be on high alert for. We also learned we must anticipate and endure the next likely major phase—a bone marrow transplant.

Naturally, I had to Google the word nadir in the context of this strange world of chemo. It turns out that adults in chemotherapy hit the nadir within ten days after their initial treatment. Adults are typically given a break before the second dosage to allow the cells to rebuild. Normal service, as it were, is resumed in twenty to thirty days in an adult body. A child's metabolism is different. Often, shorter timespans prevail—both in reaching the nadir and rising from it. Why, then, might anyone—why might Louis Unger—need a bone marrow transplant?

CHAPTER 9: DAY NINE

My notes for November 29 look ahead to the glum possibility of Louis needing a bone marrow transplant. Going into great detail, Mary Ellen and I had already been making enquiries about the personnel in Yale New Haven Hospital who might be involved in a BMT. I had been enquiring specifically about the intensity of the procedure and its aftermath. Our experience with the leaking port had affected me. It renewed my dedication and energy. Here's what my searching revealed:

> *Amy – new to oncology not done transplant yet would be his nurse. Transplant nurses – Carolyn great resource; Angela – 10 transplants. Cindy > 10 transplants; Lucy; Carey; Cathleen; Jessica; Transplant 1 month of very intensive treatment - isolation for 2 weeks after chemo > a week of chemo – blood count low w/ platelets – to zero*
>
> *Then needs complete isolation; need to give him injection 1 per day to GCSF stimulates white blood cells in back and upper arm > May get **Bactrim** against pneumonia > Treatment of chemo depends on mouth sores and his counts – recovery from treatment. Injections of GCSF - at home - 27 gauge needles – smaller – is 29 smaller, or smaller. Prescription for Emla – start 24 hours after chemo to get.*
>
> *Opening of needle up 45° angle in plunge out – do not pull back – Mary Ellen and I [to] practice.*

Mary Ellen and I had to learn how to give injections. This was the first time since Lou was diagnosed that my wife and I actually had a real moment of stress release. We were practicing giving **G-CSF** or **Neupogen**, a colony stimulating factor injections. These injections were vital as the Neupogen would stimulate the growth of Louis's white blood cells after chemotherapy treatments. The sooner his white blood count would rise to normal levels the less likely he would get an infection and the sooner we could start the next round of treatments.

Mary Ellen and I practiced these shots on each other—that was the training the nurses recommended. Mel practiced on me and did a fine job hitting the center of my bicep. Now it was my turn. I looked anxiously at my amazing wife, worrying about stabbing her with a needle. I missed and somehow put the needle into my own finger. It hurt like hell, but it was a classic slapstick comedy moment, and we both laughed for the first time since we had visited the pediatrician. I was never allowed to give a shot to Louis after my demonstration of ineptitude.

That Thursday night, a week and a day into the catastrophe, I wrote my first treatment report for colleagues, friends, and family. I suppose, in retrospect, it shows some progress on my part that I could now express this in my own voice. Here's what I said:

> *Lou finished his first two days of Chemo and it was tough. They pump chemicals into him that will burn your skin if you touch them. Amazing that the medicine goes to the rapidly dividing cancer cells and kills them. It also kills the blood cells so Lou will have to be very careful of infections when he gets home – which will hopefully be on Saturday.*
>
> *Today he was in great shape and had little nausea. He has to do all kinds of hard things, like swallow pills, wash out his mouth with 3 different solutions. Mary Ellen and I learned today how to give him injections, which we will have to do after he gets home. I accidentally put the needle through my finger when I tried to practice on Mary Ellen. We laughed for the first time in a while. Things are improving, although still we cry a lot. Every day is a great day.*
>
> *Lou, Harry, Mark and Mary Ellen.*

CHAPTER 10: DAY TEN

Mary Ellen had slept in the hospital every night since day one, inches away from Louis. I had run the home front, holding down the base—with Harry watching everything from a most difficult vantage point. This was our new normal. My wife and I were always concerned about both our boys and years later I asked Harry how he had felt about this difficult time: "It was hard not getting as much attention as my brother," he said, " and there were absolutely times I felt jealous of him—which sounded as dumb then as it does now. I rarely saw my mom for weeks at a time, and there were times I was scared, and missed her more than anything. But I don't blame my mom or dad. How could I? I realized then—and more now—that taking care of Louis was a massive undertaking alone."

On day ten of this ordeal, November 30, 2001, Mary Ellen and I continued to ask questions and track all the procedures. We made sure we knew the names of the personnel involved at any level. Here are more of my notes, which show the level of detail I felt necessary:

> *Lou doing great this morning: Meet Dr. Van Hoff at 2 pm.   Will get unit of red blood tomorrow morning: Platelets: Sunday, Mon, etc. Nuclear meds **MIBG**. Scan Monday:*
>
> *On Sunday – mix w/ OJ - Iodine solution blocks thyroid: 3 drops every day through Friday: Check PD Radiology – 2nd Floor: Scans take 1 hour: PD Specialty Clinic on Monday – 2nd Floor Access Port: Scan times are from Monday injection: 1 Tue: 1 Wed: 1 Thursday: **Nuclear scan** – 30 min to hold still: Empty bladder Get Iodine – keep in fridge: Could use this to tag neuroblastoma cells.*

Dr. Jack Van Hoff, a pediatric hematologist and oncologist, working alongside Diana Beardsley, administered the next scan, known as MIBG—its full name is meta-iodo-benzyl-guanidine. The Children's Oncology Group definition says that such scans "help locate and diagnose certain types of tumors in the body." It's a scan that works especially well at locating the presence and spread of neuroblastoma.

Dr. Van Hoff was tasked with directing his technician to release a small dosage of radioactive dye through the intravenous line into Louis, which would act as a tracer. Then, within twenty-four, forty-eight, or perhaps seventy-two-hour intervals Louis would have to lie still under a painless scanner, and have pictures taken as the scan traveled down the length of his body. We hoped the doctors and radiographers reading the scans would not see bright spots—because those would be cancer cells.

Even though none of this would happen for a few more days, Dr. Van Hoff and others outlined the procedure to Mary Ellen and me so that we could be mentally prepared. Since Louis was about to be discharged as an outpatient we also had to learn how to administer certain treatments at home. Though painless, the medics said, these procedures were not entirely simple, nothing radioactive ever is, and Louis would have to take a supplementary, iodine-based medicine (mixed with orange juice) to protect his thyroid gland. We understood that accumulating too much radioactive iodine can damage the thyroid gland—and pile more stress on a patient.

They conducted an MIBG scan twice over the space of two days. Typically, four hours after the dye is first introduced through the IV line, the patient lies under the machine, which comes down close but never touches. Scary for a small child, though, but Louis would have mild sedation, principally to ensure stillness. The first pass takes about half an hour, and the next, on the following day, takes up to an hour and a half, with no dye injection in advance for the second scan. One note I took shows that I had located in advance exactly where the scan would take place, how long it would last, and what medicine Mary Ellen and I would have to give Louis at home. My next note, however, reveals a new and important development. I had begun a serious conversation with an expert on neuroblastoma at Memorial Sloan Kettering Hospital in New York City.

Saturday, 1 December:
Cleared to go home at 2pm. Phone discussion w/ Dr. Kushner at Sloan Kettering

– Lou arrives at home – doing great – playing outside & having fun. Went to sleep at 9.30 after good dinner – Temp. OK – Theresa sleeps over w/ Evan – good to be w/ Harry.

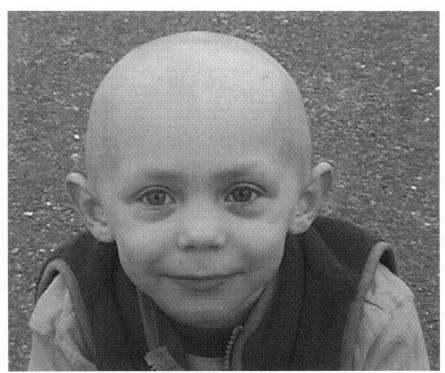

Louis is looking and feeling great

CHAPTER 11: DECEMBER 1, 2001

Louis Unger came home on Saturday, December 1, forty-four days before his fourth birthday. Before leaving at two o'clock in the afternoon, the hospital continued with its efforts to keep up Lou's strength, as I recorded in my notes:

> *Received red blood cells overnight & platelets in the morning; and to balance the forces of chemotherapy: GCSF injection given at 12:0.0 No sign of rejection.*

We felt we deserved to cut loose just a little and relax. My sister, Theresa, and her son Evan, came to stay with us from Utah. We all felt like our family had been reunited after a long and terrible dream. Life was almost normal for some wonderful hours and days. Louis was allowed to play in the yard, as he always had. Harry had his family together again under his own roof.

Mary Ellen and I had almost forgotten this life; we were now transported back to where we were two weeks ago. We got our favorite greasy Greek pizza from our favorite diner, chatted at the dinner table about Harry's days while we were gone, rented a movie, ate popcorn, and pretended all was normal. We cuddled together in our bed at night to read stories and be close to each other. We were a family again, if only for a few days. We enjoyed our time and the bond we had together.

Now, however, even though we had been playing with a deck that everyone said was stacked against us, we were home and Louis was with us, doing well. We had already come a long way very successfully.

But what did all this add up to really? That we had cleared some fence in a never-ending obstacle course? Maybe it was the first, maybe the last, who could tell? What were the odds now? Louis was in treatment, would go on receiving chemo, and our efforts would continue. However, for these two days, for this weekend, we were all breathing more easily and relishing our familiar environment again. It was just a little ease, a soft armchair, a safe harbor for a moment.

Yale New Haven Hospital had brought us to this point, but I felt determined to research beyond our local facility and see if there was a place that specialized in exactly what we now knew Louis had—neuroblastoma. I searched for online support groups, clinics, and doctors specializing in the area of neuroblastoma. I compiled a list of names, phone numbers, and addresses. That very weekend, I had made a phone call that would lead to a major change in our lives. I called and spoke with Dr. Kushner from the Memorial Sloan Kettering Cancer Center. Dr. Kushner took this unexpected weekend call at home which impressed me immediately.

In my mind, Phase One had ended. Privately, I was left wondering how many phases were yet to come. Mary Ellen and I would never give up, of course. We would fight long and hard to keep Louis alive and get him back to full health and a normal life. However ferocious this disease could be I took comfort in the fact we were a tight, strong, determined family with untold reserves of perseverance.

A few days earlier, the hospital had shared the results of a skeletal survey. The report began with "Clinical Information: Stage IV neuroblastoma. The patient had a history of left-sided Legg-Perthes disease and continued to have hip pain. On follow-up films, lytic [disintegration] lesions were seen in the metaphysis [widest part of a long bone]. Further evaluation revealed an abdominal mass. No prior skeletal surveys for comparison."

The report went on to discuss the skull, the pelvis and spine, the legs and arms, and concluded that such lesions as were detected were "compatible with the patient's known diagnosis of metastatic neuroblastoma." Bottom line: the cancer had damaged Lou's bones.

I always braced myself for more bad news when handed a report; however, there was nothing new here. I penciled notes all over the report— observations, queries, comments. On the back of the next sheet of paper I noticed some scrawled marks across the page. There were the letters, "L-O-U-S" written large, and obviously scribed by my son. Under these letters were five simple round faces. First, a smiley face; then, a less smiley face; then a straight, grim line of a mouth; then a downturned mouth; and finally, a face with a downturned mouth—and teardrops. It was the pain meter used by the hospital for kids to express their level of pain. I wondered what his level might be as he drew his name on the page.

We continued to take careful care of Louis and I faithfully took notes so we would keep track of our required duties.

Sunday 2 December: Nurse arrives at 10:30 to give injection. Lou very brave. Continues to play. Family comes over. Stay positive & short- term oriented.

Receiving iodine drops. Nice evening w/ all – hectic.

We created a home hospital. If I'm tired of all these needles, jabs, and skin punctures how must Lou be feeling? Given how many adults fear injections and must look away, what about a small boy? Lou was very brave. He was so accepting and uncomplaining. He led the way in terms of attitude. The iodine drops I put on his tongue are in anticipation of the nuclear MIBG scan planned for Tuesday. We continued to grind this out.

At home, when everyone was asleep, I would retreat to my small downstairs office and begin doing research and reach out to the world of neuroblastoma. There was a vast amount of knowledge on the web that I started to tap into. I created lists of the top neuroblastoma institutions with the names, phone numbers, and email addresses of their leading oncologists. Data and medical reports on treatment options located on government websites were stored in my files. I collected addresses of support groups for children and families afflicted with cancer—the information was vast and overwhelming.

The number of neuroblastoma patients treated by Yale in the last year constantly rolled around in my brain—two, only two. I decided to focus on the most urgent need first: finding the hospital and doctors that were the world's experts at treating neuroblastoma. Two sites struck me as essential reading: NANT.org (New Approaches to Neuroblastoma Therapy) and MSKCC.org (Memorial Sloan Kettering Cancer Center). The time for action was now, so at one in the morning I started to pave our path for the next 5 years.

I wrote to doctors in Philadelphia, San Francisco, Harvard, Michigan, and all over the United States. Here's the body of my e-mail which also serves as a summary of this story so far:

Dec 2, 2001

Dear Dr. XXX,

On Wednesday before Thanksgiving our 3-year-old son, Louis, my wife and I went to visit our pediatrician because Lou was not feeling well. He had been diagnosed with Legg-Perthes in August of 2001, and since early November he had lost energy, complained about more leg pain and stopped eating.

New X-rays showed the Perthes at a normal stage, but spotting of the Femur was of great concern to the Radiologist. Our visit to the Pediatrician on the Wednesday turned into a horrible rollercoaster over the next 10 days. Lou was diagnosed with Anemia and sent immediately to the Yale Children's Emergency room.

Soon we were on the oncology floor talking to Dr. Diana Beardsley, the Attending Dr. on call. She explained that Leukemia was likely, and that further tests would provide a diagnosis. On Thanksgiving we were told the tests were negative for Leukemia, and that a tumor in the abdomen was another possibility. The hours of waiting in uncertainty were the hardest of our lives.

Urine tests and a CAT scan were ordered. By Friday afternoon we had the primary prognosis – stage 4 neuroblastoma. The CAT scan showed a tumor in/near the adrenal gland and the urine metabolites were 10x the normal levels. We were devastated and unsure of what could be done. We were relieved that we now knew what Lou had.

On the 24th, a portacath was implanted, and further bone marrow tissue was taken to ensure the neuroblastoma cancer and to determine its markers. The next 3 days were filled with base line tests and scans and continual discussions with the doctors. My wife, Mary Ellen, and I began to learn about the disease, the possible cure, survival rates, blood counts etc. Life as we knew it changed.

On the 27th chemotherapy began according to the Children's Oncology Protocol A3973, a relatively new protocol. The chemo was tough but went well. Lou was feeling much better by Friday and was released from the hospital on Saturday, December 1. When he left the hospital he was already neutropenic.

We are happy that treatment has begun and very glad that Yale is only 25 minutes from our home. Our 5-year-old son can visit his brother and play with him after school. Many friends and relatives have given me advice about other institutions that specialize in neuroblastoma, and I am now speaking with the leading doctors to find out about more treatment options for my son.

Yesterday, I spoke with Dr. Kushner who explained the Sloan Kettering protocol to me. This discussion was of great concern to me, as it created uncertainty about our current course of treatment. He was also kind enough to give me your name for further reference about treatment options for this horrible disease.

Our family is concentrating completely on my boy's battle against neuroblastoma. We have a family pact to get Lou better. The responsibility on my wife and me is great, as we are overwhelmed and uncertain about what we should do. The decisions we make over the next months will, with God's will, save our son.

Please contact me as soon as possible at our home [telephone number given]. I would like to discuss my son's condition, treatment and the best way for us to move ahead.

I will also try to contact you over the next two days.
Thank you in advance for your help and advice.
Mark, Mary Ellen, Harry and Louis Unger.

PS: I have attached a picture of our brave Louis on his second day of chemo.

At 4 am, I had completed all the emails and reflected before heading to bed. The leading neuroblastoma doctors in the world now knew about Louis and we would soon have more information and options to consider. I had no idea what to expect or if I would receive any answers.

Morning came quickly and our new normal life continued.

Monday, 3 December – go to hospital for injection of radioactive dye for scans on Tue/Wed. Got platelets due to low count. Needs to come in Wed. 10 am for blood count if possible – see how his marrow reacts. Normally 10 days after last dose of Chemo counts come up. Mom tried to give a shot of GCSF > did not go well.

The following day, Louis needed another platelets transfusion. Our illusion of a quiet family week at home came to a rapid end. Like marionettes, we were mastered by forces beyond our control.

Slowly, we grew to understand what our new life was to be.

> *Tuesday, 4 December. Quick hospital visit for MIBG Scan > 11 – 11.30 > Harry coughing & sneezing - has viral infection – likely to go to Lou > fever likely. Nurse gave him a shot.*

The fact that Harry had become ill worried us greatly, of course. Any infection or virus would spread quickly and easily to a child undergoing chemotherapy.

> *Wednesday – All day hospital visit > back to hospital until neutropenia goes to 500 > currently very low –*
> *1.15 MIB6 scan 2:00 pm back to Center > Lou spikes fever – looks bad – throws up – Fever to 101.5 – sent to floor – **Septra** & **Vancomycin** – 2 separate antibiotics – if blood is clear then drop one. May need another blood draw location to test if port is infected or not. Blood 6 level of 100 is normal – 96 level – 100 – Had heart rate of 146 – 100 is normal. Fever settled.*

When we got Louis into the hospital at Yale on Wednesday morning for the second scan, his white blood cell count at 500 was heading toward the floor.

The Children's Oncology Group describes **neutropenia** this way: "White blood cells fight infection. A normal white blood cell count is between 5,000 and 10,000 cells. A white blood cell count below 1,000 cells increases the risk of infection."

The risk escalates when the count drops to below 1,000, and any number around or below 500 constitutes high risk of infection. That's where Louis was: 500 or 0.5—and with a fever spiking at 101.5°. The medical staff at Yale New Haven ordered Louis back to the Pediatric Oncology floor where he would have to stay until his fever broke and his white blood cell count returned to over 1,000 or 1.0. antibiotics were administered at once—Septra as a standard, to deal with wide infection possibilities, and Vancomycin. Meanwhile, I asked about every phase of every treatment—and kept records.

On it went—the treatment to correct the treatment, and the treatment to correct the side-effects of the treatment correcting the treatment. Treating this degree of illness, medicine is a world of action, reaction, experience, and experiment. My notes now included, for the first time, the classic side-effect of chemotherapy: hair loss.

Dec. 6 Continues to get Septra & Vancomycin for pretrial infection

Dec. 7 Hospital stay continues – white count same – Dr. Van Hoff says that MIBG scan did not bond to the NB cells – results not helpful = this happens in only 10% of NB cases – need to review previous M1BG treatment protocols.

Dec. 9 White count to 0.2 – Lou losing more hair.

We learned quickly that the effects from the harsh chemo were equally harsh. Lou felt terrible and had begun to spike a high fever above 103. His blond soft hair began to appear on his pillow and in our hands as we stroked his head. The level of continuous care for our child from Mary Ellen and the amazing nurses and doctors happened around the clock. IV bags were replaced constantly as Lou received hydrating fluids, red blood cells, platelets, three different antibiotics, nausea medication and Tylenol (acetaminophen) in stages for his fever. The activity and level of care was dizzying.

Lou and Mary Ellen in treatment.

The initial burst of medical activity we got when Louis was admitted was relatively light when compared to this all-hands-on-deck, 4-alarm fire reaction. We didn't fully realize it during our first round of chemo, but we learned that Louis's life was on the line. An infection with a depleted immune system can just as easily kill a child as the cancer.

My wife stayed with Louis most nights and I would go home to be with Harry. We both stayed with Lou during the day to manage and learn from what was happening to our son.

I would pick up Harry from the bus stop and made sure he was cared for, gave him all of my attention, got us both a good meal (normally take out), helped him with his homework, had a good talk, and read him a story before he went to sleep. We talked a lot about Louis and how he was feeling.

Mary Ellen and I had come up with a way to explain what was happening to Louis that cut through all the medical lingo. There were good and bad cells and the bad cells were attacking the good cells. We were now mustering an army inside Louis to wage a battle to kill and destroy all the bad cells. We were fully committed to this war and it had to be won. Both our boys loved to play with tanks, guns and other weapons so we knew they would understand and relate to this reasoning. They did. We talked a lot about visualizing the bad cells and shooting them with artillery, guns, and arrows. The battle for Louis's life had just begun.

After Harry was asleep, I returned to my office to continue my relentless work. First, I checked my inbox and was surprised that many of the doctors I had written to had already replied. I don't know why I was surprised, but I know I was really happy to start reading their responses.

All the responses contained detailed, helpful, thoughtful, and compassionate advice. They suggested: various clinics; doctors, and hospitals; and lists of drug trials, protocols, and treatment histories. The names of these doctors, and their recommendations began to surface in my notes as I tried so hard to find answers.

> *Q&A – Specific results for CAT Scan: MRI: Bone Scan > Metastasis to Liver? Kidney? (Shimada histology) – open biopsy – biological characteristics i.e. needed Tumor biology; Shimada histology N-myc gene amplification:*

"Shimada," referenced in this last set of notes, is Hiroyuki Shimada, a graduate of Yokohama City University School of Medicine. Working at the Children's Hospital attached to the University of Southern California in Los Angeles, Dr. Shimada is a pediatric endocrinologist, and a world authority on the pathology of neuroblastoma. My note deriving from that contact, "Shimada histology N-myc gene amplification," refers to a prognosis tool. The N-myc gene (now called Mycn) can be found in tumors.

One of Dr. Shimada's (and his colleagues') many contributions to the clinical study of neuroblastoma is a discovery showing that by combining features of histology and patient age at the time of diagnosis, one can increase the precision of identifying high-risk neuroblastoma. In other words, Shimada improved the previous system that uses the human genetic structure as a tracking device. This greatly improved doctors' chances of assessing and forecasting a young patient's survival.

I also spoke by phone to Dr. Katherine Matthay, a pediatrician in San Francisco and took these notes:

> *Early tumor removal not proven> Best to remove tumor after max shrinkage*

> *Make sure not to lose a kidney or to wait too long for next treatment*

>Lou's tumor is large, but not unusual - Is it wrapped around blood vessels?

Dr. Matthay explained some of her procedures in California and I noted the following:

SCSF does Vaccine therapy with MIBG prior to transplant if the Cancer does not respond to chemo. Study also done at Philly. MIBG scan is important to have. Boston has a good facility > Recovery from first chemo can take 14-18 days. Feels Yale is a competent facility and close to home. Open for further discussions and advice. Nice lady to speak to.

Encouraged by learning so much from Dr. Matthay in our phone conversation, I continued to widen the range of my search and made these notes about Penn, the University of Pennsylvania;

*UPenn: **Carboplatin**: Cyclophosphamide: Doxorubicin: Etoposide: Cisplatin: **Ifosfamide** > Tumor removal: Stem cell transplant*

*– **myeloablative** Chemo > possible double **Irradiation**: 13 – Cis-retinoic acid – 6 mths*

Dr. Berthold in Germany confirmed much of what I had already learned recently. I received a six-page document from him and made notes while talking to his secretary on the phone.

Dr. Berthold. German leading specialist in NB: Spoken to Secretary – will review my e-mail and get back to me: Send him PDF file for Protocol MIBG – technische problem '84: 1979 – Antidorpen > GMCSF: Retinsame? In between: CO6 – protocopisgut: Tumor can stay/un operable: Renoola

My goal had been fulfilled beyond my imagination. I had received so many data points for treatment options and best practices from various specialists. I felt overwhelmed by the generous outpouring of help. I studied my notes over and over again. One image kept appearing in my mind. There was a survival chart on the MSKCC web site that told a remarkable story. It showed graphically what the survival percentages of neuroblastoma patients had been over the past twenty years. It grabbed my mind and did not let go.

Soon, I developed a tentative sense of how to go forward, and on the recommendations of many, specifically the online neuroblastoma group, I copied down directions to the Memorial Sloan-Kettering Cancer Center:

61st FDR left – A Block on 61st – RT onto York – North
6 Block – "A" elevators to 3rd Floor.

This is the address of a building complex on the eastern side of midtown in New York City that overlooks the East River by the FDR Drive. These buildings comprise what is considered by many to be the leading cancer hospital in the world.

CHAPTER 12: DECEMBER 11, 2001

Memorial Sloan Kettering Cancer Center began in 1884 as the New York Cancer Hospital at 106th Street and West. It was the first institution in the United States devoted exclusively to the treatment of cancer. From its early, modest seventy beds for patients it expanded its size while testing every significant surgical and medical development in the treatment of "Cancer and Allied Diseases."

In 1939, Memorial Hospital moved east across the city, onto land donated by the Rockefellers. Nearby, a decade later, Alfred P. Sloan of General Motors, and his head of Research, Charles Kettering, funded the opening of the Sloan Kettering Institute for Cancer Research, the world's first such laboratory. Finally, in 1960, came the announcement, "[to] More efficiently and effectively to apply advances in the laboratory to the treatment of patients in the clinic, Memorial Hospital and the Sloan Kettering Institute incorporate to become Memorial Sloan Kettering Cancer Center." However, construction and expansion continued, and now Memorial Sloan Kettering has the standing of a world brand name in cancer medicine.

I first became aware of Sloan's expertise with neuroblastoma patients in December, 2001, when I found Dr. Kushner's name and spoke to him on the phone. Dr. Brian Kushner, a graduate of Johns Hopkins Medical School (class of 1976) is one of the pillars of Dr. Nai-Kong Cheung's Neuroblastoma Department at Memorial Sloan Kettering. Connecting with Dr. Kushner introduced me to two facts that I found powerful:

First, Sloan Kettering gets a majority of the 300/350 diagnosed neuroblastoma cases in the United States every year, and parents from all over the world have been bringing their children to Dr. Cheung's unit for years. By comparison, like most hospitals, no matter how excellent, Yale New Haven might see no more than two or three cases annually, and had nothing more than a general oncology and hematology department with which to address the disease.

The second powerful fact was on Sloan Kettering's website. A powerful chart burned into my brain that proved Sloan Kettering's success rate in keeping children with neuroblastoma alive was 50% and possibly more, whereas COG protocol, used by Yale, ran around 25% to 30%. These statistics pointed the way forward.

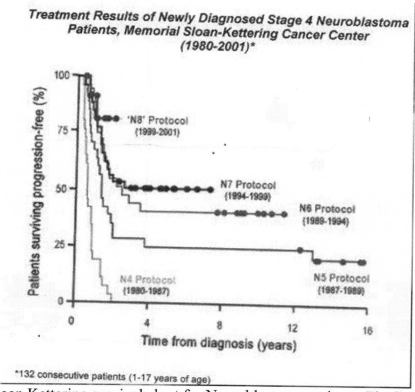

Treatment Results of Newly Diagnosed Stage 4 Neuroblastoma Patients, Memorial Sloan-Kettering Cancer Center (1980-2001)*

*132 consecutive patients (1-17 years of age)

Sloan Kettering survival chart for Neuroblastoma patients. The lines indicate the long term survival for each protocol Sloan Kettering has used. Louis was on N8

One other factor would also influence our decision for future treatment: Sloan Kettering, while advancing in all kinds of unique and independent directions, was working on the eighth version of the neuroblastoma protocol called N8, a generation beyond N7. They had started more than twenty years ago with N6.

On Tuesday, December 11, 2001, three weeks after the catastrophic news broke about Louis, I drove ninety minutes to meet with Dr. Kushner in New York. As you can imagine, I typed up a list of questions. I gave Dr. Kushner a copy so that we could work through them together and literally have the same agenda. My questions included the following:

Our son was neutropenic for 8 days after chemotherapy CDV – is this unusually long?

He is getting GCSF shots daily to boost white cells – bone marrow was taken on Nov 24 – no NB Marker results to date – done at Michigan – is this ok from a treatment point of view?

Our son's MIBG scan did not show a correlation – how is this possible?

You mentioned [on the phone] operating as soon as possible – how do you determine when?

Would you be willing to give us another opinion and act as a part of our treatment team?

Would you be willing to advise Dr. Beardsley?

What are the key differences between Sloan's Protocol and that of 3973 we are currently on?

If we adopted the Sloan Protocol would it be randomized and for what parts of the Protocol?

Is there a way for us to keep the proximity of Yale (family unit) and get the know-how of Sloan – i.e.: Transplant treatment, advice, Antibody Therapy? Distance makes Sloan impractical for daily visits.

Is the Sloan Protocol exclusive to Sloan or can you share experiences and Protocol with Yale?

How can we best utilize Sloan's experience with NB while keeping our family intact?

Specific treatment questions:

What do you and Sloan believe > single or double [bone marrow] transplant?

Is your chemo treatment similar to the COG Protocol – do you use different chemo drugs?

What trials do you currently have open for recurring NB?

*Study on (MABs) **Monoclonal** antibodies (Trojan Horse) by Dr. David Scheinberg? When would this study open? What are the eligibility criteria? They are using this in Germany for a while, what does the German research show?*
What do you think of the Dendritic Cells protocol at U of Michigan?

What do you think of the 131I-meta-iodobenzylguanidine treatment from Germany?

T-Lymphocytes treatment of the G(D2) tumor?
Wormwood Plant extracts?

Sitting in Dr. Kushner's modest office full of books, we worked through my questions. "The treatment for neuroblastoma, high-risk neuroblastoma, spreading all over the body, is very intense. You see the children constantly, almost daily, for weeks at a time, for months at a time," said Dr. Kushner, quite simply.

"Any cancer that has spread is generally considered incurable—the curable cancers are the ones that are localized. That's why parents can be extremely distressed, and feel guilty. Because once things have spread, it's very, very hard to cure. I'm not just talking about neuroblastoma; I'm talking about cancer in general. The thing that stands out about neuroblastoma is this—usually, at the time of diagnosis, it already has spread all over the place. You can't catch it early," he said, calmly. "In a sense it's two major forms. It's the kind that both stays localized, and is extremely curable, usually with just surgery, not even radiation or chemotherapy. Or it comes fully formed, so to speak, where it's all over the place. And big time. So it's not like, 'Oh, we've got to look hard to see if it has spread.' It's so obvious when it has spread everywhere—and you have to kill every one of those cancer cells. That's the huge challenge."

Dr. Kushner keeps extraordinary notebooks on his patients—small, black-covered, densely annotated pages, in tiny, spider-legs writing. He has scores of them, stacked high in his office, which also stores the bicycle he rides to work every day after his typical rising at half past four in the morning. He also keeps a different kind of record—a large, dense, binder, which documents a comprehensive medical history of each patient.

"I started about the same time as Dr. Cheung, in the late eighties. Our goal was to cure one child. It's an explosive disease—in other words the children can be well today, and a week later they're in bed, in pain and with bumps going out of their head from the spread of the tumor. Awesome problem."

I originally found Brian Kushner's name via the ACOR (Association of Cancer Online Resources) ListServ. To visit the neuroblastoma ListServ platform boosts one's faith in humankind—the general tone of the posts is a mixture of sympathetic understanding and firm, practical advice. Numerous responses to my questions mentioned Dr. Brian Kushner and generally pointed me in the direction of Memorial Sloan Kettering. Comments were made by parents, family members, and those who had been through or were in active treatment all over the world. The neuroblastoma ListServ was an enormously powerful resource throughout our battle with this monster

And so I met Dr. Brian Kushner on Tuesday, 11 December, 2001. His white coat was a bit rumpled, his dark hair a bit matted, and he gave me the impression of a genius professor. His eyes had an intensity and compassion that gave me pause—what had this man seen over the past 20 years? His words were precise and filled with confidence that had been earned through experience. I realized immediately that this man was a consummate professional who only treated neuroblastoma patients. Our conversation lasted about twenty minutes and I recall how open and direct he was. Here are my notes:

- *Very open to talk to me and about Lou's treatment. Confident in their treatment achieving 50% success rate.*

- *Follow their protocol precisely and have continuously improved their treatment*

- *Current Protocol is N8 with antibodies after 3rd chemo*

- *MYCN amplification is important more in relapse since the cancer is more resistant. Treatment is the same for all markers for Stage 4*

- *Sloan does comprehensive testing on all patients. They do a biopsy of the tumor to detect typing and to keep tumor cells for future potential treatment*

- *MIBG test is important for further treatment with vaccines. Note MIBG 131 is the test we did. It normally lasts 2-3 days. The MIBG 123 test is more sensitive and only lasts 1 day. Boston or Sloan good facilities for this treatment*

- *Surgery is very important after 3rd cycle*

- *Have best surgeon. Normally begin next treatment within one week after surgery*

- *Want to move fast and with experience gathered*

- *Don't purge the stem cell harvest, since they get good results. If harvest shows NB cells, they postpone and harvest after next therapy.*

- *Do lots of stem cell harvests – Need 5 for treatment and get 10-15 in their harvest.*

- *Do not randomize the treatment in their study*

- *Begin Antibody therapy after 3rd cycle*

- *Only have 5 courses of chemo before transplant*

- *Need formal enrollment to receive treatment*

- *In all cases can get Antibodies at the end of treatment to mop up.*

- *Also use VP16 orally after transplant to help mop up and kill NB*

- *Do bone marrow test after 2nd Chemo to test*

- *Can use Sloan for major treatments and keep Yale for rudimentary tests,*

- *Not as good as working with Sloan directly, but can work*

- *Need to follow up with Mary Ellen and Dr. Beardsley.*

- *Took a tour through facility. Reception area is rather crowded and hectic but organized with free food and drinks for all. Clowns and Shrek were visiting kids.*

- *The solitary rooms were quiet and nice with TV's and amenities*

- *Had at least 6 NB patients being treated*

On the drive home, I kept mulling over this new information and weighing our options. My mind often wanted to drift in spirals, but I had to develop a clear line of logic to discuss with Mary Ellen. Here's a sample of the main facts that I held in my head during this drive: Sloan uses a protocol similar to something two iterations ahead of Yale New Haven's COG; Memorial Sloan Kettering doesn't belong to the COG protocols; it develops and monitors its own protocols; **MYCN** amplification is important more in relapse, since at that point, the cancer is more resistant; and treatment is the same for all markers for Stage 4.

By the time I pulled into my own driveway I had worked up a few more burning questions: How effective will this immediate chemotherapy treatment at Yale prove to be? Will Yale be able to get rid of the tumor on Louis's adrenal gland or will that need surgery? And what happens after that? What will cure him?

I ran the risk of creating more questions than answers. Before giving a full accounting of my meeting with Dr. Kushner to Mary Ellen, I had to remember that Dr. Kushner had presented some very promising answers. I learned that Sloan does comprehensive testing on all patients. Sloan does a biopsy of the tumor to detect typing and keeps tumor cells for future potential treatment.

And still the reality was that the tumor sat inside Lou's body, possibly growing all the time, like an alien creature. Yale told me that chemotherapy would shrink the tumor. However, Dr. Kushner told me surgery is very important after the 3rd cycle of chemo. Sloan has the best surgeon. Sloan wants to move fast.

Up to now, surgery to remove the tumor had not been mentioned at Yale. (In the COG protocol to which Yale subscribed, surgery only took place after five rounds of chemotherapy; in Sloan, after three.) Dr. Kushner had said not to purge the stem cell harvest. If the harvest shows NB cells, they postpone surgery and harvest stem cells after the next therapy. He had recommended we do lots of stem cell harvests

As I sat in my car in my driveway, I quickly came to the conclusion that Sloan Kettering was a different world, a world that only battles cancer and one that even has a unit specializing in conquering neuroblastoma. They treated nearly sixty new neuroblastoma patients per year. I felt a pull towards moving Lou to Sloan.

Knowing that a longer haul faced Louis than we had hoped, I continued to put the facts together and build a case for moving Lou. One fear I had had was that Sloan was focused on testing new treatments and therefore did not treat all patients with the same care. Experiments require control groups to receive placebos. However, Dr. Kushner reassured me by saying that they do not randomize the treatment in their study. He said there were no placebos, no separated groups chosen at random, in which some are given the treatment the doctors are banking on, while other patients receive the appearance of treatment that amounts to nothing.

Nearing the end of my initial meeting with Dr. Kushner, I was reaching for a solution that would allow Lou the best of both worlds—the convenience of Yale, near to our home, plus the benefit of the huge Sloan expertise.

After our talk, Dr. Kushner gave me a quick tour of the Pediatric Day Hospital (PDH), where most of the treatments would take place. He explained that patients and their parents would arrive in the morning, receive treatment, and then go home in the afternoon. No inpatients would be treated here, instead they would move to the 9th floor of the hospital above.

Parents and their children were set up in rows along the outside of a large open room. Each family had their own individual space divided by standard hospital curtains. Each space had a bed, chair, and a TV attached to the wall. This was a very simple and bare set-up.

The PDH was all business with nurses moving quickly between curtained-off spaces administering care of all sorts. It was designed for maximum efficiency. It felt cramped and overcrowded as though the patient count had outgrown the space. There was a small playroom with all types of toys, books, and video games where kids could hang out. A small kitchen area had coffee, juices, and snacks for the families.

Although much encouraged by my meeting with Dr. Brian Kushner, I was still seeking reassurance that moving to Sloan would be our next best move. Mary Ellen listened eagerly to all I had to say about Sloan and my meeting with Dr. Kushner. It was such a huge decision to make. We gave ourselves a little time to sit with all the facts and impressions. I was leaning towards Sloan being the right place for Lou, so with the intention of getting my hunch confirmed, I wrote the following to the Neuroblastoma Online Support Group;

> *Our 3 year old son was diagnosed three weeks ago with Stage 4. We started treatment at Yale under the COG protocol. After the initial treatment we have started to research other facilities - Sloan, Boston, Philly all being regional to us. We found Yale to be very competent in administering treatment, but not experienced in treating NB, with only 2-3 cases per year. We then visited Sloan and were impressed with their team and dedication to fighting NB, as well as their results. We are considering moving to Sloan and wanted to get some feedback from anyone who went there. Issues, such as responsiveness to questions, communication about treatment, availability of doctors, compassionate treatment vs. being just a number, nurse's niceness to kids, and any other pros or cons would be helpful.*
> *We appreciate your frank replies.*

The **ListServers** responded immediately, and with a strong consensus. The parents of children currently being treated at Sloan strongly recommended it. I had already heard from Dr. Kushner about the antibodies that were part of their treatment plan and now parents were confirming that this was a major breakthrough treatment available exclusively at MSKCC. I didn't know exactly what these antibodies were but it was clear no one else in the world had them.

There were a few responses that suggested alternative hospitals, and one discussion has stayed with me forever. It was with a parent who wanted to talk off-line or not in the public domain of the list- serv. I had a short, personal phone exchange with a parent whose child was in

71

treatment at Sloan. He said that their family's decision to be treated at Sloan was based on the experience and survival statistics first; and secondly (and for me most strikingly) that should their child not survive, they could never second guess their decision not to go to Sloan. They never wanted to face any guilt or doubt that they had lost their child because they didn't give him the best chance for a cure. Even if our son didn't make it, the father told me, we would know in our hearts that we did all we could.

I had never entertained this line of reasoning, but I found it compelling and emotionally wrenching. To lose our Louis was not even on my radar. Now, I stopped to absorb what I had been told. How horrifying to lose a child to a dreadful disease and then second guess oneself for the rest of one's life. We wanted to give Louis the best chance for survival on earth—there was no question.

We decided to get another opinion from Dr. Germain, our pediatrician. In a phone conversation, he expressed our situation and dilemmas very clearly—sacrifice our family life for a year or more for a 20% better survival rate. What would our family life be like without Louis? The decision was clear.

The next day, I wrote the following to Yale.

December 13, 2001

Dear Dr. Beardsley,

Per our phone conversation today, we have made the decision to follow the Sloan Kettering protocol for the treatment of our son's neuroblastoma. Attached is the information requested by Dr. Kushner for the transfer of Louis to Sloan. We also request a copy of this information be sent to our attention at our home address for our records. Our intent is to continue the treatment per the Sloan protocol, with the next Chemo round administered at Yale. Further treatment would take place at Sloan. We welcome a close cooperation between Sloan and Yale so as to make routine treatment possible closer to home, when feasible.

Please contact Dr. Kushner directly if you have any questions or issues as to the information they have requested. [Contact information was included.]

We deeply appreciate your dedication and treatment of our son, and look forward to working with Yale when possible.

Best regards, Mark D. Unger
Cc: Gregory Germain, M.D.

CHAPTER 13: DECEMBER 14, 2001

The month of December continued as it had begun: Louis in the hospital at Yale New Haven; Louis at home; Louis at Yale; Louis at home. A transfer to Memorial Sloan Kettering wouldn't take place until the end of the year, or early the next year. We continued monitoring Louis carefully, and I didn't like what I was seeing;

Wednesday, Dec. 12 – NMYC number info not processed correctly (or wrong amt. of marrow sent) in Minnesota. Repeat samples sent.

Results awaited. Fish marker – southern blotting MIB6 – showed negative – did not know what type of test was done – ordered the results sent to Office for forwarding to me > Need another scan!

Dec. 13 – White cells comes back to 9 > OK for release – decision made to move to Sloan

Dec. 14 – Lou home – doing well – dealing w/insurance

Insurance! Over every moment of every catastrophic medical experience hangs a sword, maybe a guillotine—the money. I knew this was costing a huge amount but how much? How was I going to pay for it? Were we going to lose everything?

Within minutes, the cost of any hospital experience of any complexity runs up into hundreds, then thousands. In Louis Unger's case it would become multiples of seven digits. We are not a poor family and we have health insurance, but I had no idea how all of this treatment was going to be paid for. I knew that in the end it didn't matter as we would spend our last penny and borrow what was necessary to get Louis the best treatment we could.

In the United States, every illness that requires contact with a hospital or more than one doctor creates financial anxiety. With notoriously astronomical medical bills, and health insurance companies infamously strict and profit-driven, any length of time in a hospital bed, especially if unanticipated, becomes fraught with worry. By now, in the third week of

Louis's confirmed diagnosis, we felt financial pressure and creeping fear.

Sometimes, what you don't know can be a blessing. What we didn't know at that point was that because neuroblastoma is classified as a rare form of cancer, many procedures were still categorized as "experimental" by the Food and Drugs Administration. Unless the FDA has approved a therapy, the insurance companies will not pay for it. In addition, moving Louis out of the state of Connecticut, where our insurance had its focus, must, without question, have raised a red flag. We knew enough to know it was time to get some professional expertise in this area.

I called Michael Strouch who was our company's insurance broker. The old saying, "Your insurance is only as good as your broker," rang true for me. Mike and I spoke about my situation and he informed me that our insurance was restricted to in-state hospitals. We had renewed our policy on December 1 and I never paid much attention to in- vs. out-of-state insurance. Now I was in a panic. We could not go to Sloan Kettering with our current insurance.

Mike told me to stay calm and he would see what he could do. He came back to me the next day and told me this news: Blue Cross had decided to retroactively change our insurance to an out-of-state policy and Sloan was covered! My wife and I wept for joy-a hurdle we didn't know existed just a few days ago had been cleared.

Insurers classify a case such as Louis's as "catastrophic," which means more than the fact that the sufferer has been hit by a catastrophe. It means that this patient now has the potential to cost the insurer huge amounts, especially if the illness has arisen from a rare disease, and needs consideration outside the norms. That's where the broker can play a valuable part. Mike and I worked long and hard on the financial realities of this illness.

All through December, the plans for Louis clarified; he would complete the second round of chemotherapy at Yale and then, when transferred to Sloan Kettering, a further round (Sloan, remember, stipulated three rounds before operating on the tumor); and then surgery, followed by a bone marrow transplant which was a must if we signed on for the N8 Protocol.

To manage the remaining chemotherapy rounds at Yale meant intensive home nursing, most of which fell to Mary Ellen. Here's how she describes this period of care in her own words:

"It was crazy. I think he had to have medications four, six times a day. There was mouth care three times a day; it was almost constant care just making sure everything was right. It's very, very complex, the aftercare, and we had some visiting nurses come by. Plus we were struggling with learning how to give injections and trying to avoid them by getting the nurses to do it for us. It was very, very intense and it was from morning to night."

She added how hard it is "to stick a needle into your three-year-old child, harder still when the child is made so fragile by cancer and cancer treatments, and harder too when you have no medical background, and your experience consists of sticking your husband once for practice."

Louis continued to be the perfect patient through the home care phase following his chemo rounds. He rarely complained and was always brave for any painful medication or needle sticks that were required. We bought him a remote control tank that fired missiles and made machine gun sounds. He loved to play with his new toy and kill bad cells with the weapons aboard at every turn. His smile and laugh reminded us that he was a beautiful three-year-old boy who just wanted to play.

Typically, it's the mother who does the home care; statistics say that women form a significant majority of home-carers. Fortunately, I was able to take leave from my company and help, thank goodness. My responsibilities at our family business were broad and international in scope since I managed our European business in Germany and the UK. During the first days of treatment I let my two brothers and business partners know what was happening. I stayed in touch with my direct reports via phone and email, but my mind had shifted away from the needs of the business.

After discussing the situation with my brothers, Jan and Dane, and firing an employee without real cause, I decided to take a leave of absence from my day to day work. Trusted employees assumed my responsibilities and I was fortunate that my brothers picked up the rest of the slack. I tried to stay in touch with my team when I could, but let them know that I needed them to take on more responsibility while I was tending to my son. They performed exceptionally. Cleared of all work responsibilities, I was able to focus 100% on what lay ahead.

Mary Ellen created a great system. Here's how she described it: "We made this chart of tasks— of what we had to do for Louis during the day. Whether it's giving him drugs or mouth care to prevent the sores—there was a whole list of things, and we were busy all day long, caring. It was very complex, and we were completely on. I think my brain was crackling with energy the whole time, because I did not want to miss one single thing, even if it seemed insignificant—I just felt that a lot of insignificances could pile up to be significant. I knew that I had to get every single thing right—I didn't want to miss a dose."

In such an intense home-care circumstance, there's not much help from anywhere. What is available can soon become an economic matter, because even a supportive web of broker and insurer has limits. Mary Ellen described the situation perfectly:

"We had a visiting nurse coming once a day to inject him, and that went on for about a week until the insurance company really started pushing us to start doing injections ourselves—which is like stabbing somebody. It was a big mental leap to make—not having any medical background."

Louis slept with us. Mary Ellen believed she woke up perhaps every hour or so to monitor our son.

"I think the only time I could feel anything would be that first moment when you wake up in the morning. Until you remember where everything is in your life you wake up and you feel good. And all of a sudden, it all just hits you. The whole weight of what you're going through comes on you. And you load up for the day and then just go with it," Mary Ellen explained.

After more days of low platelets, transfusions to counter them, and some further contact with Dr. Kushner at Sloan Kettering to keep the way forward paved and level, the second round of chemotherapy was scheduled to begin at Yale on Monday, 17 December;

Meet Dr. Beardsley – platelets low

@ 48 Needs 75 > Dr. Kushner at Sloan Dec. 20 – Counts good to go - chemo starts 3am after hydration > According to Sloan protocol – similar chemo > Problems w/ nursing at night – IV location also difficult - threw up overnight

While the chemotherapy continued in the hospital setting, Louis tossed and turned his way through restless nights, and then on 23 December Yale released him to go home, and he became an outpatient again in time for Christmas.

People can be so very kind. Mary Ellen remarked that the children had tons of presents that year. And not just from us. Different organizations brought us so many toys that we simply couldn't give them all to our kids.

One of the detectives from the Fairfield Police Department lives in Bethany, his son is the same age as Harry, and they always collect toys for kids at Christmas. They brought us two giant bags full of toys. We picked out a few things that we thought they'd really love, and donated the rest to the toy closet at Yale.

Even an arch-competitor to our family business sent toys, and all through November and December, balloons and teddy bears and candy piled up. Despite all the kindness and excitement, Mary Ellen's memories of Christmas Day itself were not happy:

"Louis's blood counts were so low, his white counts, that he couldn't be around anybody—except immediate family. So, on Christmas Eve a couple of friends drove up, and we stood on our front porch, and they had a drink with us. They brought us some holiday food and things like that," she recalled.

I slept all Christmas Day and Mary Ellen cooked a turkey. Mary Ellen remembers the day this way: "But the turkey was awful—not cooked enough! It was just not a good day! I mostly lay on the couch and watched TV with Harry. I thought it was strange. Harry chose a show with an interior designer explaining how to make various Christmas decorations. Looking back I understand it was his way of taking care of me."

After Christmas, the same rhythm came back, the same troubling, worrying, distressing cycle of low blood counts, with, now some rougher twists.

December 28:

9.00pm – Louis starts to have signs of fever

10.00pm Fever reaches 100.5 and rising. To E.R. for hospital stay > Abdomen is extended and firm – has cramps and pain. Do X-ray >But no obstruction found.

Dec. 29: 12.30 on the floor and throwing up & diarrhea

2pm cultures so far negative – no more fever > giving only one type of antibiotic now

3pm – everything is doing OK > concern over bounce back of PLTS (platelets) from infusion on 12/28 > By midnight

the PLTS count was 12 for the infusion this afternoon >
Lou takes a good poop with lots of gas and asks for food >

5pm > Crackers – feeling good 99.5 temp

6pm >Antibiotic due now & CBC due

9pm – Eat 7.30 Drink 10.30 8am wake MIB6 9am >Bone
Marrow –

2.30 – take 4 sites > 48-72 hours to get results > Urine >
Chest X-ray

CHAPTER 14: JANUARY 2, 2002

And so ended the year 2001. It was a year of terrible change for our family. Mary Ellen and I completed the transfer to Sloan on January 2, 2002, after Louis had been through the second chemotherapy treatment at Yale New Haven Hospital.

The period prior to the move was another roller-coaster. Louis had a fever. We made a dash to the Emergency Room at Yale New Haven Hospital. Louis experienced stomach cramps for no apparent reason at one point. Less than twenty-four hours later Louis had no fever, his digestion was efficient again, he was asking for food, and he was taking only one antibiotic.

The degree of isolation that Louis needed to endure made none of us happy. Harry wanted to see his younger brother, but the hospital prohibited visitors. It's difficult to defend sterile conditions and restrictions to a boy aged five (even if he was going on six). It's completely anti-intuitive to say, no, you're not allowed to see your younger brother. So a prank surfaced. A prank that makes us smile even now.

In all hospitals, there is that respiratory illness season from fall to winter. During this time, no children are allowed to visit. Everything has to be disinfected and everything has to be sanitized. Typically, the Unger family obeys rules . . . but nevertheless, we broke one.

While Mary Ellen was spending time with Lou at the hospital and I was at home with Harry we talked on the phone about somehow getting the boys together. Suddenly, I was inspired with a crazy plan. I said, "Okay, we're driving to Yale, I'm going to put Harry in a suitcase, and I'm just going to wheel the suitcase in, right? Nobody's going to know. I'm going to wheel the suitcase into Lou's room, and put it down. And then, when I pop it open Lou's going to be surprised" Finally, some fun!

Harry remembers it well: "Oh, we walked in with the suitcase. We went up to an empty floor, unzipped the case and I got in the fetal position and crawled in. He zipped me up, pressed the button—I remember him talking with the doctors, there are like doctors in the elevator and we were really nonchalant and we got out. He rolls me in the room, opens up the case, and Louis is so happy. He was fantastic!"

Nobody saw us coming in. We had a private little event in our private room. We laughed and smiled together and it did us all good. Actually, the nurses came in and they thought it was great. The nurses kept the secret for the evening. I like to think this story lived on after our time at Yale and has generated additional laughter and smiles.

As a last measure, Yale New Haven Hospital harvested from four bone marrow sites, froze the cells, and then took both urine tests and X-rays. We hoped that things could only improve for Louis now that he would be in a new hospital unit whose sole mission is to cure the disease that has attacked him.

Differences between a general hospital and a specialized unit showed at once. Sloan Kettering, always nailing down data, took bone marrow biopsies and liquid **aspirates** from four sites, two in the back near the spine and two in the front of the pelvis (where you can feel the pressure of a belt). In those days Yale New Haven Hospital only did biopsies and never took liquid bone marrow.

We had entered a different world.

CHAPTER 15: JANUARY AND FEBRARY 2002

The next month, when Louis became a patient at Memorial Sloan Kettering, our first order of business was to sign the N8 Protocol. It listed every step of our treatment for the next twelve months.

Everything was spelled out on one page in a very small font. The side effects and potential dangers covered another two pages, which we considered irrelevant. Every treatment could potentially do damage to multiple organs, cause long term side effects, or worst case kill him. We turned to the last page and both signed the document.

My note-taking decreased for a time. I felt so confident and happy about the quality of care Lou was getting that my first notes at Sloan Kettering were all about overview, the future, and survival rates. Here's a sample:

Jan 9 '02:
Dr. Cheung > 14 yrs at Sloan & active w/ NB > Goal for N7= 75% . got 50%>Goal for N8 = 80% - shoot for more> Currently they have a new chemo agent administered @ transplant that goes to brain to kill NB in brain - Antibody in trial since 12 years gone through stages of testing > Works well to attack NB cells & body's own immune system will attack antibodies. Wait for body to develop antibody so immune system is primed for attacking NB cells > Antibody also attaches to G2 cells at nerve endings > Therefore it is painful – treatment of pain and morphine > Antibody does not go to brain > No long term side effects of antibody.

Currently treat 70-90 patients in '01– most patients are relapse from COG protocol and are being treated for relapse. Have 20 new diagnosed patients on N8 - Lou could be eligible for this – but will go on protocol N8 > MIBG scan done at 9am-10am Bone marrow biopsy at 2pm – wake up 2:50 Start of chemo round 3 Cie – cisplatin & VP16 [Etoposide] on 9 Jan > Cisplatin runs w/ Miannitol to flush kidneys >6 hrs after Cisplatin is given > must urinate a lot.

Our son had now become a patient at one of the great cancer hospitals of the world and that fact gave me considerable relief. He had entered the care of people who, for fifteen years, had been thinking about no illness other than the rare and savage disease affecting my son. Nai-kong Cheung, into whose overall care Louis had now arrived, had founded the unit in 1987, when the treatments were extremely limited.

As Louis, Mary Ellen, and I acclimated to our new environment it was immediately clear that we were surrounded by the A-Team of neuroblastoma.

The staff only treated kids with this disease and therefore had no competing tasks. The daily routine was established quickly: every morning, Lou and all the other patients would get a finger stick, which meant every patient would be touched by a special finger pricking tool that would make the prick fast and almost pain free. The kids picked their own super hero Band-Aid of choice. This daily blood sample would tell the doctors how the patients' blood counts were, prompt transfusions when necessary, and give both the doctors and parents a daily update.

Later in the day, we would meet with Dr. Kushner in his office, where he would check Louis's vital signs, discuss the treatment plans, test results, answer questions, and chat with Louis. From the beginning, our relationship with Dr. Kushner was exceptional. He and Louis would joke with each other while he was examining Louis—looking for any problems or issues from the previous day's treatment. He would answer all our questions and be very unemotional about what lay ahead and what we could expect. He carried a small black book where he kept notes about Louis—what he wrote we never knew, but it was his way to track everything about Louis chronologically. Years later, Dr. Kushner told us that he had filled multiple black books about Louis.

Naturally, I wanted to meet Dr. Cheung, as soon as possible since he was in charge of this unit and this was soon arranged. Physician-scientist Nai- Kong Cheung focuses on the engineering of antibodies and immune cells to treat solid tumors in children. He has a MD from Harvard Medical School and a PhD from Harvard University. He is a pediatric oncologist who specializes in immunologic approaches for the diagnosis and treatment of pediatric cancers. His main focus is the treatment of neuroblastoma. As you might expect, he comes across as austere, formal, and focused. He sat across from me with hands folded, courteous and patient, while I asked him about how his knowledge of immunology had informed his thinking about neuroblastoma.

"**Immunology** was an obvious area, because here you can take care of things using the immune system which is your own. And it's specific. And it has a memory. Those are classic things that now we talk about. But back then, people didn't think about them as much. We learned from all the vaccines that came before us. We learned that these things are very effective. So that's what I said; I said, 'I'm going to do something about this, I'm going to make a change'," said Dr. Cheung.

Naturally, I wanted to hear him say he could cure Lou. However, I knew very well that many research scientists consider it impossible to "cure" cancer because it is so diverse and mercurial. It is always mutating and there are so many different types of lethal disease gathered under the heading of cancer.

I knew the basics. We all have the natural power of cell division—it's how we grow, go on growing and survive, and our genetic motherboard controls our cell growth, advising when to regenerate, when to replace cells that have died. Cancer cells borrow from that remarkable system. However, cancer cells are the dark side of the system. Cancer cells not only mimic the multiplying gifts of the good cells, they do it better.

That, of course, is a simplistic explanation, and Dr. Nai-kong Cheung reminded me that nothing about cancer may be considered simple, not least what its core cause might be.

"Obviously, I think we know a lot more about cancer today. In fact we know, I could say, probably a hundred times or a thousand times more than we knew thirty years ago. But do I really know how cancer comes about? I can't speak for every cancer, but I can say that for most cancers that I know it's much more complicated than we think. It's not one gene disease. You might think that, maybe, yes, a patient has this one mutation, and therefore he or she has this cancer. Yes, occasionally you do have that.

Yes, in fact some cancers do have that. But cancer is a very heterogeneous disease. That one gene is what you know. There are a thousand other ones that you don't even know. It's a life force with many mutations. And it keeps changing in time and space. So this is the lesson that we learn: cancer is something that's going to be evolving with time and obviously with treatment."

I eagerly absorbed all the information possible from this erudite man. I learned that childhood cancers are very different from adult cancers. Childhood cancer is probably related to random events during the development of an individual. It takes a lot of cell divisions before a person is fully formed and things can go wrong. Usually, cells die off when things go wrong. Once in a while, something goes wrong, and when it does that cell has the possibility of becoming cancerous.

A regular cell will divide and divide until the tissue is formed. The cancer cell doesn't stop dividing. A cancer cell spreads. So normal cells divide for a certain amount of time but they don't break off from where they are and go somewhere else. Cancer cells are different. They divide endlessly; they can get into the bloodstream, go somewhere else, and start growing in a new area.

During my numerous talks with Dr. Kushner and Dr. Cheung they both reassured me that parents have done nothing wrong by not bringing in their child sooner. Neuroblastoma just happens. It seems to be just a random thing. No one has ever found anything in the environment that caused it.

In fact, all doctors and scientists associated with cancer seem astonished that with millions of cells dividing all the time, things don't go wrong more often.

With two cycles of chemotherapy at Yale New Haven Hospital behind him, Lou began chemo at Sloan. Naturally, I was right there, keeping notes:

10 Jan – Day 1 OK – no problems – ate well

11 Jan – Day 2 more nausea

12 Jan – Day 3 more nausea increasing

13 Jan – Lou's Birthday Cisplatin only - nausea increasing > Adavan seen as effective at controlling nausea > But side effects cause "drunkenness & sleep" Other meds not very effective

Birthday boy or not (he was now four years old), the level of attention to Louis had changed, but of course, the essential problem had not. This was still a small boy who had a rare form of cancer. During every treatment and every visit to Sloan, I continued to ask numerous, wide-ranging questions. The questions now focused on the imminent removal of the tumor which was scheduled after the third round of chemo.

On 26 January, I wrote to the Neuroblastoma Online Support Group:

Hi there:

Lou (NB4- neuroblastoma stage 4) finished Round 3 of chemo (Cisplatin round) 18 days ago. The bone marrow biopsy was still positive for NB. This caused postponement of the stem cell harvest. Do you have any experience with how many rounds it takes to clear the BM? Should we be concerned that the BM has already gone resistant? Won't talk to Docs until Mon. so we are anxious.

from Mark (Dad to Louis)

Sloan Kettering had already decided that the tumor should be removed, because surgery after the third cycle of chemo was their policy. Their testing had shown no significant additional shrinkage of Lou's tumor. They wanted to remove the heart of the cancer as soon as possible. The doctors' thinking was simple—get the tumor out after it has been attacked by enough chemo to shrink it by a third, or more, of its original size. Hopefully, the tumor has been completely or mostly killed, making its removal easier. Importantly, the thinking was that the tumor is the mothership and continues to send out cancer cells as long as it is in the body. This was totally in line with what I learned from my online enquiries and other medical contacts.

Dr. Kushner had given us a surgery date for Thursday, 8 February. On the day before, carrying a list of questions, We sat down with the entire surgical team, led by Dr. Michael La Quaglia, who had been recommended enthusiastically by several of my doctor contacts across the country. Michael La Quaglia is the head of the Pediatric Surgical Service at Memorial Sloan Kettering, a team that performs more pediatric cancer surgeries than any other institution in the world; more than 500 procedures each year (ten a week), in patients ranging from newborn to young adult. This unit has special expertise in performing large, complicated surgeries, with particular experience in surgery for neuroblastoma.

Here are my notes from that meeting:

*Meet surgical team – tumor removal – put in **Broviac***
Where & how large is incision? What will be resected?
Danger to kidneys – how large?

*Remove **lymph nodes** – what is their purpose: long term effect?*
How long is surgery/ When does it start?
Any effect on metastatic remote areas after surgery?
Any effect on local areas in spine/ bone marrow?
What is gross total resection?
Who will be operating?
Limits on activity post-surgery?

We sat across from Dr. La Quaglia in his office realizing this would be one of the most serious and dangerous parts of Louis's treatment. Dr. La Quaglia was a middle-aged man who was humble and spoke softly. He had done these surgeries for twenty years and was known around the world as the best neuroblastoma surgeon on earth. It was clear he was a busy man and knew his craft very well. He had resected tumors from children that other surgeons said could not be removed. We knew that Dr. La Quaglia had a special gift that he would use to save our son's life.

This is how Dr. La Quaglia described his work to us and he filled us with a mix of confidence and gratitude: "The surgery that we do is really an exercise in knowing the anatomy in three dimensions. The nature of neuroblastoma is that it starts way in the back, where the blood vessels are. And it tends to wrap itself around those blood vessels and encase them. You simply can't take all those blood vessels out because you would be losing vital organs—the liver, the intestines, the kidney and so forth. So you have a problem in three dimensions where you have a vital freeway of blood, a major artery or vein going through the tumor. And so you have to be thinking in three dimensions. Where is the origin of that? Where is the end point? How does it course? And so it's a three-dimensional puzzle in a way. It's an intellectual puzzle. You must picture where you can cut, where you can't cut. And then identifying the blood vessels, getting them out of the tissue, tracing their course and then unfolding the tumor from around it.

"For me it's a large space when I'm looking at it. I know that, for instance, ball players would look at a baseball and it will look to them like it's a pumpkin or something. I think it's just a matter of training yourself to be in that environment and being comfortable in it. A lot of our patients are under five. We go from really newborns to early twenties, because they have the kind of tumors that we take care of, the embryonal tumors that occur in children and adolescents."

He went through Lou's specific procedure and answered all my questions with precision:

> *Operating room on 2nd floor - Wait 1st floor – update every 2 hours > Transfer to recovery room > Will be on breathing machine – intubated > ICU – Cornell via ambulance –to 5th floor > Will look puffy & bloated for 3 days >Tube in nose too >24 hours sedated after surgery > Catheter for urine > Catheter for pain in spine epidural > Chest tube for 2-3 days> Thoracical/abdominal resection from center of stomach to center of rear ribs > Thursday pm – modified bowel poop meds – 4pm, drink laxative > Antibiotics > Thurs > 1pm 2pm before bed/get up & wash w/in 48 hours > Anaesthesia ? access mediport > Combo of IV & intubated – 6.8 > 4.3 cm tumor >50-100 surgeries / year > 4 kidney removals.*

We walked out of the relatively short meeting having heard all the words but having understood little. There was too much information, even for my notes. Some things were surprising like moving Louis across the street by ambulance to Cornell Medical Center. We decided that we were in the best hands possible and would deal with the future moment by moment. We were very happy to find out that Louis's tumor had shrunk from the original 6.8 cm to 4.3 cm due to the chemotherapy, which is what Dr. La Quaglia was hoping for.

At 12:30, we gave Lou our goodbye kisses while he was receiving his dosage of sleepy medicine before surgery. He had turned four years old three weeks ago. He looked so frail and vulnerable on the adult gurney. Lou had lost twenty pounds from the effects of the three doses of chemotherapy and his rib cage bones were visible when he undressed. His spirit was as strong as ever, but he refused to eat as his appetite was suppressed due to the constant nausea. Mary Ellen and I held hands as we saw him pass through the double doors to the operating room. We hugged and cried in anticipation of our son going through eight or more hours of surgery.

Friday 8 Feb., 2002:

11:15 arrive at clinic

12:30 Lou goes into surgery

3:15 Line placed – Broviac

4:45 Incision made for tumor

9:00 Call notifying us that they are closing

9:45 Dr. L. comes out 10:30 Move to Cornell

11:30 On ventilator at PICU

12:00 Go home

On February, 8, 2001, Mary Ellen and I waited in a waiting space, while Michael La Quaglia worked on our son. We had expected a procedure lasting eight to ten hours. People in such spaces share a common routine and set of rituals: sitting; waiting; reading a magazine; holding a book but not reading it; standing up; pacing; going to the bathroom; staring out a window; and sitting again. When a white-coated doctor enters the waiting area, every pair of eyes locks onto him or her. Mostly, the doctors speak to someone else.

Mary Ellen recalled that from time to time during the La Quaglia surgery, the operating team sent a representative, like a social worker to the waiting area. "It's not what you think either, it's more like a lobby for the hospital, and it's not like a private waiting room or anything. The waiting area is at the top of the escalators from the main entrance on York Avenue. Everyone entering and exiting the hospital goes through this area to the main block of elevators."

We waited there in that public space for ten hours, and every two hours somebody from our team would come out to give us a two-minute everything- is-fine update. Finally, a nurse came out and said "He's fine, you can see him now."

"We saw him actually, before they moved him. And it was interesting, because he looked good, because of the swelling from the surgery. He looked kind-of like he did before all the chemo started, he was more like his normal size," remembered Mary Ellen. They explained that Louis would remain sedated in the PICU (Pediatric Intensive Care Unit) at Cornell all night and that we could see him in the morning. We watched our son be loaded into the ambulance that would take him across the street to the Cornell Medical Center.

I knew the surgery was extremely invasive. They had to move organs around. And I believe, Dr. La Quaglia has said that they remove a tumor, and anything else they see, and then go up the spine and look at, and feel lymph nodes, and remove those. This is a highly critical step in the treatment. This is one of the main things that had to go right. And I knew that we had the best surgeon probably on earth doing the surgery.

Dr. La Quaglia is on record as saying, "If you try to do surgery before chemotherapy, you can get a lot of bleeding. There's good data showing that overall survival is the same if you delay surgery until after giving chemotherapy. The drugs shrink the tumor and also make it less vascular [blood-carrying] to allow for much more complete removal with fewer complications."

When we first saw Louis after the surgery, he was sedated and intubated. Dr. La Quaglia came by and told us that everything had gone well, that he had taken out everything that he needed to take out, and fixed everything that he could fix.

Dr. La Quaglia had inserted a Broviac catheter. The Portacath surgically installed at Yale had to be replaced with a double lumen Broviac. A double lumen Broviac has two rubber tubes or lines so that two types of chemo or antibiotics and blood cells can be infused at the same time which is critical for a bone marrow transplant. Naturally, these tubes need to be treated carefully and infections must be avoided at all costs. The sight of two tubes exiting Lou's body like large plastic spaghetti was very frightening at first but like everything, you get used to it. Here are the post-surgery notes I wrote:

> *Discussion w/ Dr. L.Q > removal of tumor went well – orange tennis ball size tumor > parts of it were dead/chemo was effective will check tomorrow under microscope > removal of lymph nodes around tumor & others near aorta that seemed affected > Kidney function & liver were fine no cancer seen > he got out everything he could feel.*

I noted that the tumor at the adrenal glands, when first measured by Dr. Diana Beardsley at Yale New Haven Hospital, was described as a 6 cm mass/tumor above kidney on left. If Dr. La Quaglia reported that parts of it were dead, reinforcing the impression that the chemotherapy had been effective. The rest added up to good news, too; the surgeon had been able to remove the affected lymph nodes, and, best of all, had found no kidney or liver affect.

Mary Ellen and I stayed the night after Lou's surgery at the Ronald MacDonald House on East 73rd Street. Next morning, at eight o'clock (Harry's sixth birthday) we stood by Louis's bed in the Cornell Pediatric Intensive Care Unit at the Greenberg Pavilion in Sloan Kettering. Here's what I noted:

8.00 Lou waking up and biting an oxygen tube

9.00 – all is well – breathing on his own > receiving morphine 2 mg & ibuprofen " Tramadol" 8 mg every 6 hrs works well to keep Lou asleep > Continues to have chest tube to remove fluid from chest cavity & surgery location > Has urine line in to remove urine > Has tube in nose to stomach to remove bile & other stomach fluid "NG Tube" > Has oxygen going into his nose to assist breathing > Louis's heart rate continues at 160 level all day indicating pain > Breath rate is rapid at 30-40 instead of <20 > Blood oxygen levels are good but drop to low 90's every few minutes – should be >95+ > Received 1/2 unit of blood 11 am

With so many drugs still at work in his system, Louis spent his day under the necessary spell of the after-surgery painkillers and sedative narcotics. Mary Ellen and I spent our day visiting him, and observing him carefully. The surgery, by any standards, had been long and demanding; our child, to survive, had been placed in a state of suspension.

It was the most incredible ICU. Every kid had his or her own nurse and computer monitor. It was so reassuring to know that twenty-four seven there was complete supervision with a ratio of nurse to child being 1:1. Judging the expansive view of the East River, Lou's room resembled a two thousand dollar hotel room.

Mary Ellen: "Louis was awake when we arrived, I will never forget how awful that felt— knowing he had been awake and alone in the hospital. I started whispering the text from some of his favorite books in his ear since I couldn't hold him…there were so many tubes."

There was a constant, shrill beeping adding to this surreal environment. It felt like so recently he was just a little boy in pre-school and now we were here on the edge of a strange new world.

We were regularly told he had a "stable but critical condition." "Stable but critical:" that's official language, developed and honed over the years for a purpose: to flatten the emotions in a potentially volatile situation.

The next day would be different and intense;

10 Feb '02:

Dr. L. asst. comes in. Ok to remove stomach & bladder tubes. Both tubes out – no problems > Lou feeling better – begins drinking H2O & eating

11:00 Hits fever of 104. Tylenol given – normal to have fever after surgery

12:30 Fever broken. Lou gets up to take first steps. Pain but OK. Heart rate still high at 150's but down from 170's > Ox level continues to be low 93-95 has to breathe > hard to get above 95 level

3 pm Ok to go to Sloan Observation Unit

4 pm Goes by underground route to Sloan 5th floor Observation Unit.

Walking & breathing practice continues – has pain from the incision - Broviac training started –

> need to flush 2x week to clean & dressing > 3x week, careful w/moisture

PM Fever creeping back to 37.5-38 but not more> Heart rate improving

– pain med. increased.

A mere two days later Louis had no tubes— not in his chest, not in his nose, not in his throat, not anywhere. No oxygen needed, either. He was walking, talking, and his happy, cheerful self. He had come through major surgery and had the principal neuroblastoma removed—a tennis ball of cancer. The Cornell facility returned him to Sloan Kettering as a "normal" inpatient, lying in bed, in some pain, but on a recovery path. His body now showed huge scars which were dressed twice a day, and his mother was given the task of removing the little Band-Aid-like sterile strips that were no longer needed since the wound was closing.

Within about a week, he was back on his feet and though not jumping around, he was kind of back to himself and that's pretty quick. What a miracle! It is amazing how young kids bounce back so much quicker from difficult procedures than adults. Lou was tough and although he did not appreciate or like his procedures and constant treatments he knew he was killing bad cells.

A while later, I sent a gift of whisky to Louis's surgeon. On a little gift tag, I wrote, "Best in the world at resecting NB tumors." I also attached a longer note.

> *Dear Dr. La Quaglia.*
>
> *It has been some time since you operated on our son Louis. Louis recovered remarkably well from his surgery and continues to tackle his treatment with positive energy and resolve. It is impossible to truly thank someone who has saved the life of our son. The gratitude and indebtedness that my wife and I feel toward you and your team is hard to put into words. We appreciate the personal commitment you showed to our son and our family before, during, and after the operation.*
>
> *Thank you for your dedication to your gift as a surgeon. We will forever be grateful to you and the great NB team at Sloan. We have enclosed a picture of Lou and his brother Harry on our summer vacation to Wyoming shortly before Lou was diagnosed. Please accept the small token of gratitude from me personally. I hope you enjoy it with Lou and all the other kids you have saved in mind.*

Such a well-deserved tribute—not just for the technical skill with scalpel and clamps, but for the pure dedication he demonstrated. Michael La Quaglia gave me the impression that he approached each new operation with more commitment than he had the previous one. I remain in awe of his life's work.

You would somehow expect a short break in post-surgery recovery, but there was none. Lou immediately had to get back on track for the next round of chemo. His blood counts were good, so we just kept going. Surgery constituted only one phase, one aspect of the Sloan Kettering treatment protocol or procedure. Just because the tumor had been removed didn't mean the cancer had gone. In fact, had another tumor formed, especially in the brain, we would have heard alarm bells ringing beyond our most fearful imaginings; no child had ever survived a relapse manifested as a brain tumor—but no other tumors had been detected.

.

CHAPTER 16: FEBRUARY TO APRIL 2002

With successful resection of the tumor completed, the medical task changed from annihilate, as in the surgery, to hunt and kill as in eliminating any and all other neuroblastoma cells in the body. To do this, Sloan Kettering immediately continued with Lou's fourth round of chemo. The medical team prepared us with a customized "road map" of the next step in the protocol, the N8, for which we had signed up when we started treatment there.

A document of some detail, entitled Patient- Informed Consent for Clinical Research, this road map outlined "a treatment program called N8: Dose- Intensive Chemotherapy plus Biologics in the treatment of neuroblastoma." Its opening paragraph makes the aims clear:

"The purpose of this research study is to find out if our treatment plan or 'protocol' can cure a deadly form of the cancer called neuroblastoma. In the past, most patients with the bad kind of neuroblastoma died from it, because treatments could not kill it all. The N8 Protocol includes different kinds of anti-cancer treatments. We hope to increase the percentage of individuals who are cured of this disease. The current study includes treatments that have been used in the past, as well as some new types of therapy."

This lengthy document goes on to outline the principal stages in this protocol. As a standard at Sloan Kettering they only approached surgery for a tumor after three rounds of chemotherapy—a criterion that Louis had fulfilled by way of two rounds at Yale New Haven Hospital, and a third at Sloan. Therefore he had now advanced to the next stage, the beginnings of immunotherapy—the antibody-based treatment by which Dr. Cheung had come to be first interested in neuroblastoma. And in this phase appeared the most significant terminology of all in Louis Unger's young life—3F8.

The Sloan road map describes Immunotherapy as "used after tumors have been surgically removed, when the patient has only minimal disease left (in the bone marrow, for example). This treatment is designed to train the body's own immune system to detect and destroy neuroblastoma cells that have survived chemotherapy or radiation therapy. The treatment involves the injection of a substance called **monoclonal antibody 3F8** into the bloodstream. The antibodies seek out and attach to neuroblastoma cells, and signal the immune system to destroy them."

This is where the story of my son's treatment moves into what could easily be Nobel Prize territory. The basic knowledge that our immune systems generate antibodies to fight germs has long existed.

Most children of a certain generation across the world grew up seeing the black-and-white animated films that the health authorities showed in schools, in which germs and antibodies fought bitter wars. But the ordinary antibody (if there is such a thing) won't attack neuroblastoma because the tumor is "natural," that is to say, it has been born inside the body, and is recognized as part of the body.

Somebody had to establish this fact and then discover—or invent, create, design, manufacture—an antibody that would attack neuroblastoma, something that could be fed straight into a patient's system.

What the world needed was a new antibody that could hunt down neuroblastoma specifically and kill its cells.

Nai-kong Cheung set out to find a way to trick the body into developing immunity against these cancer cells in the 1980s. His work resulted in the 3F8 antibody that was part of the N8 protocol at Sloan.

This antibody, unique to Sloan Kettering was one of the key reasons that the survival rate was 50%. The Neuroblastoma Team that had created and received approval from the FDA to use the 3F8 antibody was one of the main reasons we were here with Louis.

Dr. Brian Kushner explained how this Trojan horse, 3F8, works. I was eager to understand this critical treatment and he told me the following:

"3F8 will attach to a neuroblastoma cell, and when it does that, it serves as the signal, the license, for white blood cells to kill the neuroblastoma. White blood cells are in our bodies to kill infections, but they can also kill a cancer cell if they are directed to do so.

"And 3F8 tells them to do it. White blood cells have something on their surface that will attach to an antibody. And then the white blood cells release substances that will destroy whatever they're attached to.

"Dr. Cheung was interested in neuroblastoma.

He would take neuroblastoma cells from a human, from a person, and inject them into a mouse. A mouse would recognize the human neuroblastoma cell as something foreign. Whenever something foreign goes into a mammal, and a mouse is a mammal, it reacts against it by forming antibodies against that foreign object so that it can be destroyed by the animal or person's immune system. This was a huge amount of work by Dr. Cheung—to isolate mouse cells producing antibodies."

Within days of emerging from surgery, Louis was receiving, five days at a time, the immunoglobulin known as 3F8. We were told that the doctors would watch its progress on a scanner. The naked eye can actually observe changes of color where the antibodies attack neuroblastoma. Where neuroblastoma is not present, no such activity happens because no radioactivity shows up on the scanner camera.

Louis received the first phase of 3F8 treatment in its typical phasing of between one and two weeks at a time, with weekends off. The break after each cycle stretched between two and three weeks. In this way, he became exposed to manageable side-effects such as hives and rashes and some nausea and vomiting. The most crushing side-effect is described by Memorial Sloan Kettering with these words: "Pain is the main side effect. All patients have pain."

When the antibody hits, children of all ages scream and shriek with excruciating pain for the simple reason that 3F8 also hits nerve cells.

Elsewhere, Sloan has added, "The primary side effect of 3F8 treatment is a pain reaction requiring pain medications. Despite side effects that occur during 3F8 infusion, no long-term complications (important for a young child) have been associated with these antibodies."

The Sloan handouts do warn that the pain can last from a few minutes to an hour, and that it does need to be addressed with painkillers up to narcotic strength, such as morphine; and, in Lou's case, a habit-forming drug named **Dilaudid**. Almost two weeks after the La Quaglia surgery, I made this note observing the antibodies treatment and the nursing that it necessitated:

20 Feb., 2002

3F8 – Admin Nurse –

9.35 Benadryl by IV 15mg

9.40 Dilaudid 0.2mg

9.45 Start 20 m/hrs of 3F8 – 0.0 10.15 40 m/hrs – 0.30

10.45 Dilaudid push .2mg 0.55 10.45 80X1hrs 3F8 0.60

10.55 Dilaudid .2mg.

11.00 Benadryl 10 mg Warm packs on stomach

11.05 Dilaudid .2mg

11.10 Flush

11.20 Dilaudid .2mg

11.35 Fell asleep

When they infused the monoclonal antibodies made by mice into Lou's body, those antibodies also attached to certain nerve endings, particularly nerve endings in his stomach or legs. Lou's white blood cells attacked these cells as well as the cancer. Mary Ellen would sit with Louis in her lap on his gurney and try to comfort him by first reading, then singing, then rubbing his tummy and hugging him. I would sit across from her and feel my entire body cringe.

Sitting with our child who was in screaming pain was torture. It was torture for Louis, who had to endure the pain, and torture for us, because we could only watch helplessly while our son went through agony in order to save his life. Every treatment was similar and

Louis always, always had incredible pain. We could never get used to this pain, as you can never get used to the drilling of a cavity or the prick of a needle or cut in your finger. Only this was 1,000 times worse since the pain was our son's and we had to watch and listen to it day after day. Louis would go through over one hundred antibody treatments in all.

The way we tried to cope with what looked like total cruelty was to tell ourselves that these treatments were saving his life. Here's a sample of this relentless regime of treatment and effects:

22 Feb., 2002

8.50 IV hook-up

9.00 Benadryl & Tylenol

9.15 3F8 – 20mltrs L Dilaudid

9.45 3F8 40 ml

10.12 Dilaudid

10.15 3F8 60ml

10.40 Dilaudid – Lou asked for it

10.43 Pain starts

10.45 Dilaudid

11.05 Flush starts

11.15 Pain slows – stop screaming

11.20 Sleeping

11.30 More pain

12.00 Dilaudid

Note: 4 doses of Dilaudid provide max. pain relief, so the infusions build upon each other – though short pain relief Duration 20 mins

Give him a pill of Dilaudid on Sat.

Benadryl, even when taken as an antihistamine, carries the somewhat vague instruction: "Do not operate machinery." Benadryl makes a person drowsy. Dilaudid is a controlled substance and requires meticulous dosage and care to be taken. Through February, March and April, 2002, this treatment continued at Sloan Kettering. Mary Ellen and I came to New York, stayed at the Ronald McDonald House, and Louis courageously fought his way through the chemotherapy and antibodies. We insisted on inpatient chemo so that Louis could have IV anti-nausea drugs. They were far better for Louis.

Of course, a parent wants a child to feel as much relief from pain as possible. Mary Ellen noticed that Louis almost looked forward to getting pain killers. We would say, "Give him the full dose, whenever you can." Pain killers work, however it is very concerning because addiction is real, too. As a parent of a very young child, it was our call to say whether or not he should get another dose of pain medication. It was a very, very difficult line to walk. We both wanted to err more on the side of giving him comfort rather than keeping him in pain.

We noted that Lou's heart rate would rocket up when the pain came. It was well-documented, excruciating pain. Added to this, there were at least twenty other kids getting the same treatment all around us. This was the key treatment difference that Sloan had, the numbers of patients they continually treated. This led to their superior knowledge, improved treatments, and superior survival rates.

Hearing a chorus of screaming children was hard, but unavoidable. They had to endure pain if they were to survive.

Mary Ellen would always get there really early so that they would be first in line for the treatment. Neither of them could be called "morning people;" however, if they got there early Louis was less exposed to all the other kids screaming.

By March 2002, I felt ready and able to write an e-mail to friends and family who were all wondering how Lou was doing.

Hi everyone,

*The last bone marrow biopsy had both good and bad news. The bad news is that Lou still had cancer in his bone marrow. The good news is that 7 out of 8 tests were clear of the neuroblastoma – a good improvement over the previous test. The bitter-sweet information was hard for us to receive, but our hopes and expectations are always guarded these days. The docs see the results as a positive step towards **remission**, and we are certainly happy about the progress. The antibody treatment and continued chemo are working to reduce the cancer. Once again we are anticipating the next test after our current chemo round is over.*

Last week we finished the second 5- day treatment of antibodies. Lou came through this well, although the painful symptoms remain. Tonight Lou is sound asleep, here on the 5th floor at Sloan. He is through the second day of chemo with two more to go. We hope to be home by Friday night for about ten days of recuperation.

Lou continues to be in great spirits while his brother Harry would like all of us around more. Mary Ellen's mom has taken great care of Harry during our time in New York and we are thankful we have our mom's help throughout this treatment.

We wish you all a peaceful and happy Easter/Passover break. Lou will be hunting for eggs on Sunday.

Life continued. We traveled between Connecticut and New York, between home and hospital. On 30 March, 2002, with Louis now very frail, I posted this enquiry to the online neuroblastoma group:

*Lou has just finished his 2nd round of Cisplatin chemo. During the first round he threw up for 4 weeks after chemo. Besides the common nausea meds (Zofran, Ativan, Vistaril, **Kytril**) has anyone had any luck with anything else – homegrown or med wise? Thanks for any help – last time Lou lost 2lbs which he has not put back.*

One of the mothers online replied, as so many did, with clarity and generosity, "I remember when Josh had chemo that finding the right nausea drug cocktail was worth its weight in gold." She advised us to "experiment not only with the drugs but the increments in which they are received, and how long between doses. Josh needed more than one, and he needed them more often than they were allowed. But we found that if we broke down a day's worth, and gave him increments throughout the day, it fought the symptoms much better. Are you giving any calorific supplements?"

By mid-April, I was sharing our own important comparisons online:

We have found that the Cytoxan Chemo rounds (1, 2, 4), always put our son in the hospital with a fever. The Cisplatin rounds (3, 5) were not as severe. Since Lou has an older brother, we encourage them to play together, even keeping Harry out of school so they could be together and play. Harry misses his little brother a lot and after getting some professional help, we decided to put a lot of emphasis on family time at home. Despite lots of cleaning and bleach, we always knew that Harry could transfer viruses or infections to Lou. In the end, we figured on hospital stays for Citoxin rounds - which proved to be right every time. One of the most difficult issues we have had to face is the separation pain and anger that Lou's brother has had. As Lou will be away with Mom, Dad or both for longer periods of time, we cherish the time when we can be together, in the wonderful (almost) world of being a normal family again.

How do you parent a child in such circumstances? What do you do about the other child in the family? Who, no matter how much he wants to help in sharing the family anguish, is too young to know what's going on, and can't but feel that his younger brother is getting all the attention. Of course Lou was getting all the attention. That was unavoidable and appropriate. I cautioned myself against living in the future.

The present was no cake walk either. Time after time, Mary Ellen and I tried to see this experience through Harry's eyes. "Harry desperately missed our smiles and happiness. We were so grim, especially at home, in downtime," Mary Ellen confided to me at one point.

Mom and the boys in the hospital

We need not have agonized so much about Harry. He has gone on to be tremendously accomplished in so many areas. Recently, I asked him what he remembered about Lou's ordeals and this turbulent time when he was only five years old himself.

"I don't really remember asking questions. I'm sure I did though. They told me what cancer was, how it grows through your cells. And all those things. One of you told me that Louis was really sick and that you thought he had cancer. Oh, well, what's cancer? I read a lot as a little kid, I knew a lot about a lot of stuff. Yeah, I knew what cells were. Even though I was young, you always made it a point to explain everything to us. Because I read a lot I understood things like cells and what cancer was," said Harry, years later.

Five year-old Harry joined the "battle," as he saw it, to fight off the invaders who were attacking his brother. "I would make little Lego, like a train or a bunch of cars, cancer-fighting cars, I would get all the little Lego guys, put them all together. So this is going to go inside Louis to kill the cancer - the evil army. I was in a huge part of the struggle," he has said.

Mary Ellen and I tried very hard not to make Harry feel left out and yet not feel an enormous emotional burden all the time. Harry remembers it this way: "I remember being told, 'If you'll be a good boy right now that will really help.' There were times when he was getting toys and stuff, when I was a little bit jealous. And I knew at the time, 'Oh this is stupid. He has cancer. Cancer sucks. But I knew that Louis would be okay. I never felt that Louis was going to die or be in mortal peril."

In September 2001, Harry began to keep a journal. Children do what they see their parents doing, after all. He drew bold, expansive lines of pencil and crayon drawing on wide sheets of paper: a soccer game; a church; and early in November he drew a small flash of red chaos on a page, adding the words, "Little brother is sick." On 26 November, days after the initial cancer news broke, he made a tall and fierce drawing of angry, vertical lines in red-pink, blue, and red-orange. Behind this unpleasant image, hopeful yellow windows were peeping through. He added two words to his picture: hospital and Louis. This made it very clear to me that Harry felt upset by Louis's situation.

I asked Harry how he felt during this stressful time when he was older and he said this: "During his treatment, I tried to help out the family by being the best "good boy" I could be. It's taxing to be putting on a brave face always, and my school performance dipped. This is even before having to answer every question from my classmates. But I struggled through it as best I could, because I knew that this was the best way I could help Louis get better."

As Mary Ellen now recalls it, "Fortunately, people who were parents and sent gifts to Louis also included Harry. But so much came from Mark's business associates, people who didn't really know our family, and their gifts were all for Louis—stacks of them on our doorstep. Harry's kindergarten teacher sent Louis a gift and before he opened the box I prayed that there would be something in it for Harry too. It was a teddy bear for Louis. There were also some stickers that I told Harry were for him. But I could tell by the look on his face that he didn't buy it."

Naturally, Mary Ellen and I tried hard to put on a positive attitude each day and be as upbeat as possible, however, there were awful ups and downs from the minute Lou first saw the first doctor.

In April, we received bad news and I felt I had to be very real with everyone so I released the new and harsh information, while still remaining upbeat and optimistic:

Last week, we found out that Lou's bone marrow biopsy was still positive. The same small amount of tumor was still found in his right front hip. We had all hoped that he would be clear so he would be able to move to the transplant phase of the treatment. We were both sad and hurt by this news. Learning to cope with the anticipation and anxiety of the "testing and results" stages of Lou's therapy has been very hard. We try not to get too excited so we are not too let down - however it's impossible to fool oneself. Slowly the pain lifts and is replaced by renewed spirit and hope. Lou has had a great two weeks home. No fevers, no hospital visits. We have kept Harry out of school so the two boys can get some real brother time in. They helped Dad in the woods, Mom in the garden, played wiffle ball and rode their go-karts constantly. The family time has brought Lou's appetite back and he is back to bacon and eggs for breakfast!! This is big - there is nothing better than seeing Lou eat 3 pieces of bacon to start the day.

Tomorrow, antibody treatment begins [again]. We will go through two weeks of antibody therapy and take another bone marrow test. We will try to downplay our expectations for this one again. The wonderful support everyone has given us is simply amazing. Lou's kindergarten class families prepare and bring us a family meal once a week, family and friends have sent cookies, German potato dumplings, candy and other goodies. Lou loves them all. Daily cards and photos keep Lou very motivated. At night he always says the same prayer: "Dear God, I pray everybody is thinking of me" while looking at the pictures on his wall.

Every day is a great day!

The optimism must have worked. At the end of the month, we had reason to believe that we could at last prepare for the next, and final, phase of this frightening drama before returning to a normal life.

30 April, 2002 Hi everyone,

I am overjoyed about the final results of Lou's tests - he is finally "clear".

Although the antibody treatments were harsh, they did their job. When a 100-ton weight is lifted from our chests, the world begins to come into focus again. The huge hurdle has been overcome. Lou is cancer-free for the first time since he was diagnosed in November. Joy has returned to our hearts, and it feels good to be happy for the first time in a long time. Lou is doing great. His message on my mobile phone today was "Daddy, I'm clear! I cried for joy. We will now go through the transplant phase with Lou, which is a one-month isolationary chemotherapy. In essence, all new chemo agents will be given to Lou over five days. Following the chemo, Lou's immune system will be nonexistent. On day seven, his own stem cells will be transfused back.

Magically, the stem cells find their way to Lou's bone marrow and will rebuild it as new. The objective is to wipe out all remaining, non- measurable, cancer left in his body. The recovery period is about 21 days and any one in Lou's room must wear a mask, gown and gloves to protect him from infection. The procedure will make Lou sicker than any he has ever had, but without it the cancer would likely return. With all modern technology available, small, free-floating neuroblastoma cells cannot be detected yet must be killed. Follow-up treatment after the transplant will continue through Christmas this year. Radiation, antibodies, and oral chemo are on the protocol.

Today it all seems trivial. Every day is a great day!

CHAPTER 17: MAY 2002

Things had been going so well for Lou that we now faced a new learning curve and heard words such as stem cells, bone marrow, and transplant. We learned that an **embryonic stem cell** is an immature cell that can be directed to become any kind of cell that the body needs. We learned that an adult stem cell is a helper, part of a restoration system that will move to replace damaged or dying cells. We learned that stem cells may yet prove to have infinite medical applications. And we learned that in a stem cell or bone marrow transplant Louis would become his own donor because his bone marrow cells had already been harvested and frozen. Lou's bone marrow cells had been waiting until he was ready and able to accept them back into his body again safely.

After hearing about any next steps for Lou, Mary Ellen and I would tell each other what we understood as a way of making sure we had both grasped all the information correctly. During one such conversation, Mary Ellen said, "The stem cell transplant is essentially where they give so much chemo that they are basically wiping out the bone marrow. It's like pushing the 'reset' button on your immune system." I thought that was a good way to describe it.

On Tuesday, 14 May, 2002, I told my online community about our current situation:

> *We had the meeting with the transplant team today. Lots of harsh info to absorb:*
>
> *- After 6 days of new chemo agents, Lou gets two days "off" and then on day 8 the stem cells are transfused.*
>
> *- 3-4 weeks of recovery follow.*
>
> *- Release from hospital only after his white counts recover and he can drink normally.*
>
> *We can expect the following in short:*
>
> *- Transplant kills all remaining NB cells.*

- Zero counts for up to 3 weeks following Chemo

- Continual Transfusions of Red and White Cells

- Severe Mouth sores that require 24 hour morphine drip

- Complete loss of eating and drinking ability due to sores

- Browning of his skin due to chemo requiring regular body washings

- High fevers and antibiotic treatments

- No contact with other patients during entire period due to risk of infection

- 1 year of complete recovery to "normal" life style (school)

- No additional long-term side effects.

- Same risks as neutropenia only more severe.

Tomorrow we start. Will update you as we go. If anyone has any other practical info would be happy to hear. Lou is ready to go.

This reboot procedure made significant practical demands. Once Lou's body had been cleaned of all its existing cell support systems, he would be more vulnerable to anything and everything than on any day since he was born. Over a six-day period, a new chemotherapy infusion would more or less destroy his immune system, and everybody who came anywhere within his radius had to be as scrubbed as a surgeon, because any kind of infection through this period could prove fatal. On the seventh day, when the immune system would be at its lowest, the transplant would begin and the infection-free zone must continue for another three weeks.

"No one comes in that room without being gowned, masked and even when I'm there as his mom, I'm still completely gloved, gowned, masked— even when I'm sleeping at night," said Mary Ellen. We tag-teamed. We took turns going back to the Ronald MacDonald house to nap and shower. We spent the days and evenings with Louis. There was a lot to do for him. He needed a lot of care beyond what the medical team provided.

Waiting and watching for the new bone marrow to grow meant more blood counts, newly heightened anxiety, liquid food and questions in a locked-down environment, where even doctors and nurses do not hide the fact that children sometimes do not survive. The plastic pack on the stand by Lou's bed in his space-age room poured life-giving mixture back into our child Lou's hearing had now been compromised by chemotherapy and this hearing deficit would remain for the rest of his life.

Day after day, Mary Ellen and I waited for the next blood count, and it always seemed two steps forward and one step back, getting a little bounce in the platelets levels, and then seeing them falling again. Come what may, we were 100% confident we would beat this disease. I kept my promise and wrote an email update:

Thursday 23 May, 2002 Hi everyone,

After 6 days of intensive chemotherapy, Lou had to take 2 days "off" to get the agents out of his system. He handled the chemo very well with little nausea and a great attitude. We have all been locked in Lou's hospital room, where Mary Ellen and I must wear gloves, gowns and masks at all times. Anyone who enters the room must also be covered to protect Lou from any possible infections, viruses, and other germs. Today, Lou received his stem cells back in an uneventful transfusion.

They call this day zero. These cells will now graft into his bone marrow and start complete new production of all of his blood cells. This process takes between 10-21 days.

Unfortunately, the chemo has now begun to have its adverse side effects. Lou's white blood cell count is absolute zero and his other counts are dropping fast. He is having pain from the breakdown of his mucous system (mouth to stomach) and is already on continuous pain medication. As of Saturday, he will go on IV feeding, as he will no longer be able to swallow.

He is a trooper and holding up well. His room is decorated with dinosaurs on the walls as well as quilts and family pictures. The next two weeks will be hard, as Lou

will have no immune system and be very weak. He is
continuously monitored by a fine team of doctors and
nurses and receives the best care of all by his mom and
dad. Time will pass quickly. Every day is a great day.

One of the wall quilts I refer to here had been made by the families of his nursery school friends.

For thirty days, Mary Ellen, Louis, and I lived this weird, strained existence, always dressed in gown, gloves, and mask in a highly disinfected room. Mary Ellen's calendar for the year 2002 was filled with the hieroglyphics of dosages, blood counts, and transfusions. Now, she was tracking the most crucial data so far—the day-to-day red blood count.

Despite our understandable preoccupation with Louis, we were always very aware of having two children. Harry was on our mind a lot because he was at home without both of us for what was almost a month. Luckily, he stayed with Mary Ellen's or my mother who helped us so much during this entire ordeal. They both loved all of their grandchildren deeply and were committed to making Harry's life as wonderful as they could. They would bake cakes, take him to his various activities and read stories to him at night. Their hearts and tenderness to our boys helped us through the many nights we were not able to be home.

This was the longest time we were to be away from home and we wanted to see Harry so very much. My mother and my stepfather asked if they could bring Harry down to New York for an afternoon so we could spend some time with him. We were overjoyed that we could make this happened and Harry was scheduled to be at the Sloan hospital on a Saturday afternoon.

Mary Ellen recalls it so well: "I came down the elevator and walked to the waiting area where we had waited during Louis' operation. All of a sudden, I see Harry there, still arms at his sides almost at attention. He was wearing brand new kakis, a new blazer, shirt and tie. I ran to him and he flung himself into my arms. I held my baby for an eternity. I put him down and was so happy and proud of him. He wanted to get dressed up for the occasion and Mark's mom decided to buy him a special outfit for his visit. I cried, not only for the joy of seeing Harry, but also for the heartbreak of the fact that a six-year-old would consider seeing his parents a special occasion.

"Harry was so proud of his new clothes and hugged me so hard I thought he would never let go. He was so happy to see us and be reunited.

I kept telling him how much we loved him and that his brother was alright."

Of course, Harry could not see his brother, but he was happy to see his mom and dad after two weeks without us. We spent some time together talking about his life and what he had been up to. Of course we talked to him on the phone every day, but a 6 year-old has other activities on his mind most of the time. Now, we had each other's undivided attention. We cherished this special time as it set our feet back on normal ground far away from a hospital room nine stories above.

Mary Ellen's own medication—hope—kept rising and sinking with our son's platelets; as the levels stabilized, so did her spirits. At the end of the thirty days he would be free of cancer, the post- treatments could begin, largely at home and largely orally, and the dread-filled burden would lift off and float away. When the transplant phase ended, two more weeks of antibodies would be needed; and after that, if it worked—we would be told he was clear. I found comfort in having a community of people who understood what we were going through from a parent's point of view. My next email went like this:

Wednesday, 29 May

We are now in day plus 6 of the transplant. Lou did great until 2 days post stem cell infusion. His counts bottomed at zero, the fevers started and the mucositis intensified. As predicted by all the docs, he is very sick now. He has intense pain from his stomach and must cough up and spit out mucous every 2 hours to keep his pulse-ox. above 95. They have maxed him out on all antibiotics, he is getting IV feeding, and round-the-clock pain medication. His skin is blotchy red with dark red in all the rubbing areas (groin, armpits, etc.) and he itches the areas occasionally. He feels like crap, can speak just a few words and likes to just sleep and be left alone. It is hard for us, as we were told what to expect, but, as most of us know, it's not real until we have to confront the situation. We go hour-by-hour tending to his needs as best we can and keeping the pain under control. The docs say he is doing well - which makes me wonder what "not well" is – and that his counts should come back in 2-3 days. I can truly say that transplant sucks, now being in it. We hope to be doing better in a few days and to be done with this stage of treatment. One word of advice in all this, when your friends ask what they can do to help - during transplant lots of platelets are needed and "single donor" is the best. So we have asked friends and family - besides doing it ourselves - to donate platelets for Lou.

Just a few more days...

Warning to all visitors that hung on door of his transplant hospital room – Lou the artist

Few conditions cause as much local distress as mucositis, a side-effect that ulcerates the digestive tract and the mucous membranes. But the treatments continued, as they had to, and our hopes stayed high.

Sunday 2 June

Hi everyone,

Lou's new bone marrow started to produce new white blood cells two days ago. His counts went from 0.0 to 0.1 - the signal that the engraftment of his stem cells was

successful. His counts and his general condition will now slowly improve. Since our last update, Lou had a very rough week. Mary Ellen and I were both extremely concerned by his condition, which was deteriorating day by day. The doctors said that Lou would be the sickest we had ever seen him. Their words could not prepare us for Lou's state during the seven days following the chemo.

We are so relieved that Lou has finally turned the corner. His fevers have stopped, the pain is diminishing and he is slowly starting to regain interest in his dinosaurs again. The docs say all has gone to plan. That was one hellish plan. We are proud of our boy and his strength to get through this terrible course of treatment. In one to two weeks Lou will be released from his isolation room and we will go home. His immune system is that of a newborn and we will have to be very careful for the next 100 days. After a brief rest at home, Lou will go back for testing and another six weeks of intensive treatment. Today we are looking forward to going home to be a family again. Thanks for all of your prayers and good wishes. We have needed them all in the last 2 weeks.

CHAPTER 18: JUNE TO AUGUST 2002

As it turned out, more prayers were needed.

When the worst effects of the treatments had subsided, and a little good health seemed to have returned to Louis, we took him home for a week, knowing that we had to go back and do another bone marrow biopsy (that monster of a needle again) to see whether it had all worked.

The first test after the transplant showed he was positive for cancer. I was distraught. I felt so unbelievably angry. It was such a low point.

Naturally, Mary Ellen was also devastated. We felt we had battled so valiantly, done everything right, endured, endured, endured and then to find we were still battling cancer was crushing.

Mary Ellen remembered it this way: "It was Friday, and on Fridays we always saw the doctor, and now she said that the bone marrow test type had shown a neuroblastoma. I asked her whether she was sure it's a neuroblastoma, and she said, "Yes." And at that point the black eyes were coming back again. I was really scared. The doctor explained that that particular aspirate (the one that tested positive) was in the same area that they weren't entirely sure was clear before the transplant. So it had only gotten worse during the transplant."

Years later, we learned that the Sloan doctors had decided to stop using the transplant altogether.

The research and data showed that the treatment was extremely harsh and did not improve survival rates. So they stopped doing it. Louis was part of the data set leading to that decision. And so, from June 2002, we began again, from almost a worse point than before because we were so worn down and we had seen promising treatments not work. True, the tumor had gone, but the cancer was back in the bone marrow, even though most of the neuroblastomas in the body had disappeared.

The cancer had become resistant to the chemo. Neuroblastoma and other cancers can reproduce so fast, morphing themselves into a slightly different cell, and then no longer be affected by the current chemo agent. Think of it as survival of the fittest cancer cell. All it takes is one cancer cell to adapt itself and survive the chemo barrage and then the cancer starts growing again, except now a new chemo agent must be used.

The treatments just didn't work. We talked to the doctors. We were devastated about the results. Naturally, I turned to Dr. Kushner and here are my notes from our meeting that took place on June 15, 2002:

Previous aspirate was positive in Rt Front [hip], same as the current positive aspirate?

What is the cause of the aspirate being positive in only one location?

Why is it not positive in other locations?

You stated that it is very unlikely after a BMT to have positive NB – what does this mean for Louis's type of NB and course of treatment?

Is there any reason why it has been only in RT front on aspirates?

Is this considered a relapse?

What has been course of treatment in other patients with similar results post BMT?

Is this disease systemic and free floating in his blood stream – or localized to Rt front Hip?

Will it eventually go to the bone marrow and cause tumor regrowth?

Is the NB type resistant to the past chemo used Vincristine, Cyclophosphamide, Etoposide, Cisplatin? Transplant chemo?

What other chemo is available to treat resistant strains of NB?

What are options if next BM tests are positive? Chemo? Antibody?

What other treatments would you suggest?

Other institutions?

What is course of treatment if next BM is negative and he is clear again?

Continue as per protocol?

Risk is high that same NB will return due to return following ABMT and Antibody?

What are other treatments that could help eradicate this strain of NB

What trials do you currently have open for reoccurring NB?

Dr. Kushner had all the answers because Louis had not been the first person to relapse in his care. He dealt with my questions as he did with everything, factually, calmly, and with a wealth of knowledge based upon experience. Lou had not technically relapsed as additional 3F8 treatments were on the protocol and these could and hopefully would clear the cancer cells.

Mary Ellen and I were always amazed how anyone could seek out the job of pediatric oncologist. The cause is certainly noble and the incredible gains the doctors at Sloan and other institutions had made in survival rates for children were miraculous. But to see babies and children every day that are suffering and battling cancer along with their anguished parents must be very hard. We figured out that while most doctors cared for the kids deeply, they were also able to detach emotionally somehow. The oncologists focused on new treatments to improve outcomes and always talked about what could be the next breakthrough. These unsung heroes, hidden away in big hospitals are gifts to humanity and to families like ours.

Once we moved past the shock and disappointment, the doctors assured us that progress is rarely made without setbacks. We believed in our doctors and knew that this was the only way forward. What choice did we really have? On July 1st, Louis resumed the schedule of antibody treatments as planned. There were another forty treatments planned over the next six months.

Louis went home, and with some adjustments the routine resumed. We maintained our constant vigilance. Louis still had his intravenous lines in his body that had to be cleaned and flushed every four days to prevent clogging. We made sure that no redness developed around the entry ports. Louis and Mary Ellen went into New York every week where Lou was seen as an outpatient. I stayed home with Harry since he was on vacation for the summer. Occasionally, Harry and I would drive into New York to spend an evening together. Louis's favorite restaurant was Delizia which was only a short walk from the Ronald McDonald House on 73rd Street. All the waiters knew Louis and Mary Ellen due to their frequent visits. We loved this casual atmosphere, friendly waiters, and all the free garlic bread you could eat. No one gave Lou's bald head a second look; he was part of the Delizia family.

In July, I made a new connection online and was able to offer a little support for the first time and that felt good to do.

Dear Vinny and Family,

It hurts all of us to hear your news. The trapdoor opens beneath our feet and we fall fast and hard. The group will help give light to the tunnel ahead and open unknown passageways that would otherwise remain shut. Ask the tough questions of all of us, and you will get tough and real answers. All from parents, just like you, who are all taking their own paths. We are bound together by hardship, hope, and experiences. I am truly saddened and encouraged by every new member we gain. We, as a collective, can help each other overcome hardship, answer questions and make good decisions. If we can shine light down the trap door and join others in the experience, it won't be so frightening and we can gain confidence in choosing the best path for our kids.

Over the summer of 2002 the tension began to ease: no longer by a bedside in a germ-free zone; no longer watching blood counts by the hour. Mary Ellen reduced the family's anxiety by inviting people over, making delicious picnics, and suddenly the summer months were how they used to be. She didn't drop her guard for an instant. She never slackened her vigilance by a millisecond. Louis was still on low levels of chemotherapy dosage, now taken orally. He was still fragile after the savagery of the bone marrow transplant, its preparations and its aftermath, but he was at home, the family was united again, Harry had some much-needed attention, and the sun was shining.

CHAPTER 19: SEPTEMBER TO DECEMBER 2002

Then, one wonderful day, life became even sweeter. To our delight, Sloan Kettering said the magic word, "clear." The cancer was gone. The stubborn front right aspirate showed **NED—NO EVIDENCE OF DISEASE!** The antibodies had worked their magic, found the resistant neuroblastoma cells, and unleashed Louis's own immune system upon them—wiping them out, hopefully forever. It was nearly one year to the day when Louis was first diagnosed.

I brought family and friends up to date in a joyful September email.

After the transplant Lou had a full battery of tests, one of which came back positive for cancer. We were shocked and in disbelief that after all the treatment and hardship of the transplant, the cancer had returned so quickly. The doctors retested 2 weeks later and 2 antibody treatments later – that was Aug. 30th. We received the results back this week and were overjoyed to get an "All Clear" result. The antibodies had done their job, and the doctors decided to continue treatment per the current plan. Lou is now at home and gaining weight and hair back. He returns to NYC for one week a month of antibody treatment. Overall, he is doing very well, with terrific strength, good appetite, and great spirit. Mary Ellen and I are very relieved after the last test results, although the wait was hard, as they always are. We are now in a prolonged maintenance treatment phase. Lou will continue treatments for up to 2 years and be tested every 3 months. We are grateful for all of the continued support and love from everyone. Lou is inspired by all the people who continue to care and think about him. He is an amazing boy.

That magic word, "clear," floated in the air above our home every minute of every day—"clear." In our glorious New England autumn leaves began to fall from the trees. Louis was home, and active, and recovering. The nightmare had run out of energy. Life felt normal again. In October, Louis returned to his nursery school—and to Mrs. Garcia.

"Children are the most accepting audience. They all knew that he'd been sick, and they all knew that he was going to look different. And it just was— he's back! They were just very happy to have him there."

"He had no hair, he was a shadow of his former self, he was the same height as when they'd seen him last, he already had his hearing aids, but they took no notice. They clustered around him, with no greater fuss than, "Hi, Louis," said Pat Garcia.

Pat recalled his return to class: "It just amazes me how children do accept differences without judgment. I mean they really did treat him just like he was before. Just like one of them—it was no big deal. They had no sense of what a big deal it was. For them it was just their friend. We talked to the children before, but at age three and four they don't understand the severity of illness, they just know everybody's been sick. So we talked about how Louis has been sick, and had to go through a lot of things, and he's going to look different and he's fine, but we might have to be a little bit careful, he's still our friend, and everything's the same. To me it was important that he would be able to step back in and feel normal, to feel just like everybody else, and to be treated like everybody else— even though he went through something unbelievably remarkable."

Fall wound down. The temperatures dropped, and the colder weather in November brought back memories from a year ago that prompted me to write an update for friends and family.

Everyone,

A year ago today Louis was diagnosed with neuroblastoma. It was Thanksgiving Day and our world was turned upside down. Last week we received the wonderful news that the latest battery of tests all came back negative for cancer! Once the great news came we were overjoyed and relieved. Somehow the trickle of anxiety for the next tests 3 months from now began anew. It has been over 2 months since my last update. Lou had many infections and spent almost 1/2 of Sept and October in the hospital with fevers. One infection required his catheter/port to be removed in an emergency operation. He had a new one operated-in 2 weeks later, which is now under his skin. The antibody treatments have continued 1 week per month and Lou is on low levels of oral chemotherapy 3 x per day.

This medicine is the nastiest I have ever tasted (I taste all of Lou's oral medication to see how bad it is) and Lou is taking it without as much as a grimace. He is amazing. Lou has returned to school, when his blood counts permit. His hair is growing back - he actually needed his first real haircut last weekend - and he is steadily gaining weight. Harry and Lou are playing like brothers again. The love they share for each other is amazing. Most nights, Harry will jump into Lou's bed and they will sleep together in each other's arms - that is until they jump into our bed in the middle of the night. Mary Ellen and I feel that we have turned the corner on Lou's treatment. We feel much more confident now that we have two consecutive tests behind us, and Lou's overall condition continues to improve. We know there are no guarantees, but life is returning to normal. We are grateful the year is over, and it is behind us. All of your support helped us get through.

CHAPTER 20: JANUARY TO JULY 2003

In January 2003, after months of lighter chemotherapy, and more antibodies, Sloan Kettering routinely tested Louis again. And again Mary Ellen and I heard the magic word "clear." Now, we could believe a little further, a little stronger, that a better life was ours. I went back to work. Mary Ellen felt that her prayers were being heard. Harry was delighted to have his closest playmate around once more.

Louis himself looked less frail, less translucent. His energy and stamina kept increasing. His appetite grew. His personality blossomed.

Nursery school steadied him. He socialized. He played. He loved being a brother to Harry every day.

However, after a remission or a "clear" Sloan Kettering still wanted to check Louis every three months. In March, I wrote another upbeat email to our friends and family.

Hi everyone,

It has been some time since I have sent an update, and, as in most cases, no news is good news. Louis had his last tests and scans in early Feb. and the results were all negative. He is now in remission for 6 months and doing very well. His body has worked overtime in the past 6 months to make up for the year of treatment. He shot up 2.5 inches and has put on 10 pounds since October last year. Lou's great attitude and lovable personality is taking him through continuous treatments with ease. He is now on Accutane, a well- known acne medication that will transform remaining cancer cells to a benign state. He also continues antibody treatments one week per month in New York. Although still painful, the antibody treatments are now routine. Louis is also going back to nursery school where his teachers and classmates are happy to have him back. He also started special classes at the elementary school to help with his speech development. He has lost a lot of his hearing and now wears hearing-aids most of the time. Lou was thrilled to be able to ride a school bus home from his classes. Mary Ellen and I are regaining footing in

121

our lives and moving forward with projects long postponed. Harry is doing well in school and the brothers are playing more and more like brothers should. We continue to feel blessed by Lou's progress and face the future with more and more confidence as every day passes.

So, the nightmare was over. The disease had been defeated, and Lou, so cheerful and so resilient, had played a huge part in his own victory. How very proud we were of our son.

People who survive grave illness say they hear the birds singing with a new, sharp clarity. They find the morning sunlight brighter. Water tastes fresher and looks cleaner. As limitations continued to ease, and good humor swept through our house, Mary Ellen and I felt pure joy again. The anguish had evaporated; the anxiety had lifted; we could look out our windows and see our two beloved sons playing, and tussling, and being normal brothers.

Summer opened up for us. We were living a normal life, having a fantastic time, and doing all the normal little things again like going to the Firemen's Carnival, spending time with friends, having camp fires, having playdates with our friends' kids, and even attending summer camp programs.

Best of all, we had a Make-A-Wish trip planned. Louis, with his famous T-Rex biting toy, had always dreamed of digging for dinosaurs, and he directed his wish towards Wyoming and paleontology. When Dr. Brian Kushner asked him one day to write down his name, and write what he wanted to be when he grew up, Lou scrawled on a Sloan Kettering letterhead, "Louis. Paleontologist." Dr. Kushner keeps this page in the front flap of his thick file on Louis.

Therefore, with excitement as high as the sun in the summer sky, we planned to leave on a great road trip on the Saturday after the Fourth of July.

During our lovely days of restored freedom, we had taken our two boys on various trips. While in Chicago one morning, we arranged a babysitter, and went to a neuroblastoma conference. Paranoia of Louis relapsing was always crawling around my brain. I wanted to be prepared and continued to research the latest treatment protocols for neuroblastoma relapses. We attended a lecture where we heard a number of well-known oncologists talk about treatment options. One speaker said that from a brain tumor relapse of neuroblastoma there was no survival. That was the consensus, without contradiction. Whenever there was an incidence of neuroblastoma relapsing as a brain tumor that was the end. Unfortunately, the diagnoses for other relapses were just as grim.

After that Chicago trip, we had fun planning the Make-A-Wish road trip. We enjoyed the warm weather and often played in our backyard pool.

Being together and doing stuff together as a family was important to us. Louis's illness had impacted all of us and we knew that we should not waste our days.

"Every day is a great day" was our motto and we lived it.

On Wednesday, July 2, 2003, Harry had a friend, Julian, to visit. The three boys began cannonballing around a raft in the pool. Louis and Harry jumped on the raft together at the same time, and clunked heads. They shook it off and kept splashing.

Mary Ellen remembered what happened next: "And then Julian's mom came over to pick him up. I was pretty isolated, my being in New York for treatments so often, and I wanted to be friends with Charlotte, so I asked her to stay for a beer. We were sitting there at the picnic table when Louis came up and said, 'Mom, I got a headache, I'm going to go lie down.' I said, 'Okay.' I thought it was weird, I even commented to Charlotte. I was very anxious. All I wanted to do was go check on him, but then I had already invited Charlotte for a drink and I didn't want to seem too neurotic.

"Then Mark came home from work, and everyone got up, and Charlotte said, 'Oh I should go.' First thing I did was go inside and check on Louis. And he was out. I had no doubt in my mind. I think I was on the phone to Yale within five minutes after she left. They said, 'Bring him right down,' and we just hopped in the car. All four of us went back to the Emergency Room."

Harry also remembers what happened after he knocked heads with his brother: "I remember him getting tired. I was teasing him about it like, 'Why are you . . . Oh Louis, come on! You can't get tired now.' I remember a little bit of worry on my mom's face when that happened. It must have been at the back of her mind. She was over it. She wasn't worrying about it. And then to see that little bit of worry come back into her face when that happened that was scary as well. I mean scary . . . I didn't say I wasn't scared. I was scared. I was scared that I saw my parent's face scared."

We told them what happened about the kids clunking heads. I was thinking that maybe it was just a concussion. And they said, 'We should definitely do a CAT scan.' Louis and Mary Ellen went to get a CAT scan done.

Here we were back in the same room we had been in on Thanksgiving two years ago. Bob the Builder videos were still next to the TV and we decided to pop in the video while we waited. This time the wait was not long. The doctor came in and asked us to step outside. Without any prelude, she stated, "Louis has a brain tumor. It's about the size of a golf ball."

CHAPTER 21: JULY 2003

I had a bad feeling when we drove the twenty minutes to Yale. Mary Ellen was worried, of course, but Louis was being tested for cancer, full battery of scans, bloodwork, biopsy once a month so I wasn't expecting the brain tumor, how would that not have shown up in the testing?

Now we stared at each other again and our thoughts instantly crossed—this is bad, very bad. My mind was racing.

The roller-coaster had crashed. Our trap door opened and I was falling hard. Louis had relapsed. Not just a "normal" relapse but a brain tumor. It was the most feared of all neuroblastoma relapses. What are the chances of survival? This time we knew. We'd done our homework. We'd heard the doctor in Chicago. The fact was that no child had ever survived a neuroblastoma relapse presenting as a brain tumor. In other words, the chances were zero.

We saw the brain scan. There was a perfectly round white mass on the right side of Louis's skull. Somehow, this visual kicked me into action-mode again. I emailed Dr. Kushner from my Blackberry and he almost instantaneously replied, "Just come down."

Louis wasn't in pain and didn't complain of a headache. But Mary Ellen saw that "he would do that thing with his head which I found out subsequently was a symptom of brain tumor—leaning it to one side."

All the bad emotions invaded our lives again. No more glorious summer days. No more pool cannonballing. No Make-a-Wish, no dinosaurs, and no raptors. We were better prepared for battle this time.

They moved Lou to inpatient at Yale New Haven Hospital. I stayed with him while Mary Ellen went home with Harry, did laundry, and packed our bags for New York City. Around midnight, Mary Ellen called Make-A-Wish to tell them not to send the Wish Givers because we would not be home. Louis, she told them, was said to have a relapse, and she hoped that she could reschedule at some point.

Louis and I were back in the hospital room at Yale. He was hooked up to an IV again, getting fluids and I was trying to fold myself into a two-person couch to rest. I was wide awake while watching Louis sleeping peacefully.

My mind started to go to a dark place, where I had never gone before. I began to see Louis in a casket in front of me. I tried to push the thought away but there was nothing I could do to control my brain. I wept deeply and held Louis's hand. I opened my computer and started to write:

"Dear Friends and Family.

> *As our hearts drown in sorrow we say goodbye to our loving son Louis. He is amongst the angels now, looking down and smiling and waving to all of us.*
> *Hi Lou! He can play as a five-year- old should, free of hospitals, free of chemo, free of pain. What a brave boy you were, fighting to kill all the bad cancer cells. So brave, so wise and always ready for the next battle that we had to face. Your mother, brother and I were always so proud of your determination and grit. We love you so much..."*

The impulse to imagine this dreadful moment had been honored with these words on paper. My brain was now calm having written down the unthinkable. I was out of tears so I closed my computer and crawled into the bed with Louis to hug him for as long as I could. My determination to save our son's life had just received a painful jolt.

First thing in the morning, Mary Ellen brought Harry back to Yale and we waited for the ambulance to move us to Sloan Kettering. Mary Ellen remembers being in the ambulance bay at Yale, waiting inside an ambulance with Louis. I was holding Harry outside, and Harry was crying. Harry just kept yelling, "Louis, Louis, I don't want you to go. I do not want you to go and I love you so much!" And Louis was yelling back to him from inside the ambulance, "I love you too Harry, I don't want to leave you." For Mary Ellen, knowing what was in store for them, that they would be leaving each other for good—it was the most heartbreaking moment.

Mary Ellen said that as their ambulance pulled out, the guy asked her about Lou, and she said, "He has neuroblastoma. He has just had a brain tumor relapse, and there's nothing curative for him." And then he said to Lou, "Well, what kind of music you want to listen to?" Lou said, "I want rock 'n roll." "Rock 'n roll? You got it," and he turned it on. Mary Ellen remembers the music blasting away. It was hard rock, and they rode it all the way to New York City— with the lights on, not sirens. Just Janis Joplin— "Break another little piece of my heart."

I drove myself and Harry to Sloan. They did another CT scan at Sloan where Dr. Kushner stood, totally surprised. He did not expect this to happen, nor did the team. But ten percent of the relapses are brain relapses, and generally speaking, brain relapses were fatal. There was no cure. They could do some procedures, primarily resect the tumor. Radiation was the standard of care but they knew that would mean two, three years at best.

There was a very different atmosphere at Sloan this time. They encouraged us to go back to Yale to do the radiation so we could be close to home and family. We actually got doctors' orders to go home and enjoy the Fourth of July. Mary Ellen explained: "We decided to throw a pool party. It was definitely not a goodbye party. It was more of a gathering-your-strength party. We invited our family and our closest friends. They all showed up. It felt so good to be around people who loved us. We decided to have a good time. Lou was in the pool with his brother, and basically we lived life for that weekend. We knew, all too well, that on the Tuesday after the Fourth, we were going to ride back into the City, go for brain surgery, and face this thing."

Everybody on the neuroblastoma team at Sloan Kettering had come to know Louis Unger. To know him is to be fond and protective of him. Now, everybody on the team knew what he faced. If no relapse of neuroblastoma into the Central Nervous System had ever been cured, not ever, containment and management for the rest of his life was all that any team had ever achieved. That persistent fact always featured high on the list of Dr. Nai-Kong Cheung's concerns.

Once more, I wrote e-mails, but with a distinctly different tone this time.

July 6, 2003

To: Board Members of Germany and the USA

This message is confidential and I do not want this news to be spread throughout the company. I am sharing it with you so you understand what is going on right now. Last Wednesday, Louis suddenly had a very severe headache in the afternoon. We took him to Yale, where a CT scan showed a large tumor next to his brain. On Thursday we went to Sloan for further evaluation and the tumor was preliminarily diagnosed as a relapse of his neuroblastoma. Lou was given medication to reduce any swelling to his brain and has shown no neurological side effects. Lou is feeling very well and we were sent home over the weekend to enjoy the time together as a family, which we did. Lou spent 5 hours each day in the pool playing and swimming. It was great. We return to Sloan tomorrow to find out the course of treatment. Surgery to remove the tumor has been scheduled for Wednesday. This was a shock to us as Lou was doing so well. We now are preparing for the next battle in Lou's fight against this menace and are determined to see him through. I do not know what awaits us this week, but I will be in touch with the office when possible to conduct business as best as possible. I will be on email from the hospital and can be contacted on my cell. I am asking all of you to keep this information to yourselves until we know more ourselves and I am ready to share it with a wider circle. Thanks for your thoughts and wishes and prayers. We will need them.

Mark and family

Sloan Kettering had dealt with brain relapses before and only had a few cards left to play: surgery, radiation, and ongoing care. The problem had changed since we finished the N8 Protocol. Now, the disease was beyond their reach and outside the track record of highly successful outcomes. If the cancer had kept away from Lou's brain, he would have had a chance, with, as before, chemotherapy and antibodies. However, those treatments don't reach the brain because of the **blood-brain barrier** (BBB). This barrier protects our brain and spine from infections and disease. I learned that our spinal fluid, which circulates around our brain and spine, contains no white blood cells and therefore the barrier must keep out all threats. This includes chemotherapy which is a toxin and is not very effective in the brain. Basically, the fire brigade couldn't get to that part of the fire.

On that July day, few people in the world knew this predicament in such depth as Dr. Brian Kushner. He explained it as follows:

"One of the things notable is that neuroblastoma is almost never seen in the brain at the time of diagnosis. No one really knows why, but that's the fact. In contrast, relapses definitely can happen in the brain. The brain and spine, they're guarded from the rest of the body—an evolution to protect from toxins. It's called the blood-brain barrier. So it's possible that even one cancer cell landed in the brain somewhere along the line. You don't see it on the scan, but it would sit in there protected, because the chemotherapy doesn't get through to it. It might get through the bones and bone marrow, through the main mass - but not in the brain. And with children— as it happened with Louis—it can relapse only in the brain. Nowhere else. We call that an isolated Central Nervous System or CNS relapse," said Dr. Kushner.

The first step was to have the brain tumor removed. We were introduced to a neurosurgeon who would be performing the surgery. Pediatric Neurosurgeons are extreme specialists as they deal only with children who have brain tumors. Dr. Mark Souwadeine was the neurosurgeon that the Sloan team counted on to remove neuroblastoma tumors.

He was tall, in great shape, and had a presence similar to Dr. La Quaglia—he possessed confidence based upon experience.

We talked to Dr. Souwadeine' in his office while Louis sat on Mary Ellen's lap. He explained in layman's terms what would happen. Lou would be under full anesthesia and his skull would be cut open at the site of the tumor. He would then resect the tumor and anything he saw that looked like cancer tissue before closing the opening. Louis would have little to no pain and be back on his feet after the procedure. My wife looked at each other and both thought—that seems pretty easy—knowing that it was not.

The 6-hour surgery took place on July 9. Dr. Souwadeine removed the tumor inside Lou's skull.

Mary Ellen is very visual and creative. She would cultivate go-to images in her mind that helped her stay positive. She imagined Louis graduating from nursery school very vividly. That came true in June. But now, faced with this new situation in July she worked hard for a new visual.

While in the waiting room at Sloan during the radiation treatments, she found a famous children's book, The Carrot Seed. Written in 1945, it has never been out of print. Containing only 102 words, it is one of the shortest texts ever published for children. It tells the simple story of a boy planting a carrot seed and waiting with hope while he heard discouraging words. The little boy would not be discouraged and his determination was rewarded. The final illustration shows him with a huge carrot in a wheelbarrow. Mary Ellen, who wins horticulture prizes in her own life, felt very moved by this story. She loved the simple story of hope. She kept that last illustration in mind and would draw on it for strength at times.

We talked to Dr. Souwadeine after he had resected the tumor. He said the surgery had gone very well. The tumor "popped out" which was not uncommon in neuroblastoma brain tumors. It wasn't entangled nor had it grown into the brain which was a blessing. Our first step in battling the relapse was a success. When we saw Louis, although his head was bandaged, he was alert and talking. We had expected a similar follow-up to the one he received after the first tumor removal, but he was already ready to go home. Clearly, brain surgery had come a long, long way.

With the tumor gone, and the brave, little patient handed from the surgeon back to the physicians, Dr. Kushner was again overseeing the case. He had discussed the case with the neuroblastoma team and the next step was to begin chemotherapy with an agent Louis had not received before. Irinotecan was supposed to be effective at penetrating the blood brain barrier and it could get into the brain to kill cancer cells. This was to be combined with radiation to the brain and spine. The radiation would kill nearly all of the cancer cells. The problem everyone knew was the word nearly.

We went home and the side-effects of the steroids Louis had been taking for two weeks to reduce brain swelling were beginning to show. He was gaining weight all over his body. It was as if he was swelling or being pumped full of air. It was odd to see him look bloated after he had been so skinny for so many months.

Louis on steroids for brain tumor and having fun in the pool

Soon after the surgery, maybe a day or two after, he became very quiet and not himself. He didn't want to do anything; he just wanted to be held. He didn't talk, he didn't play, and he gradually just wanted to sleep. Lou was just not himself anymore. Through everything, he had always been a child. He always played. He always bounced back. Now he was at a point where all he wanted to do was sit and be held. He did not want to talk. He did not want to play.

It was frightening to see Lou so lethargic and we knew that the radiation was not scheduled for a week. I emailed Dr. Kushner and the radiation team to plead with them to take Louis immediately. He was fading in front of our eyes. Later Louis referred to this as his sleepy time.

Luckily, they were able to take Louis earlier, my persistent begging worked. After his first round of radiation he bounced right back. It was a miracle. Mary Ellen and I were amazed. It was as if a veil had been lifted. By the 3rd round of radiation, which was schedule every day for two weeks, he was nearly back to his normal self. The prep time for each treatment, which didn't take long, took longer than the treatment.

Lou had to lie on the table in a full body mold so he would remain perfectly still. Small pencil mark tattoos were put on his head and body so he would be positioned exactly the same for every treatment. This was a very precise science. Dr. Wolden, who runs the Radiation Oncology

Department, was very concerned about over radiating the children. While radiation is very powerful and a great cancer killer, it must be used very carefully. Too high a dose and Lou would be left with long-term brain damage. The wrong bodily position would expose the wrong parts of his brain or spine which would mean permanent damage. Louis was bolted to a very fine line.

Fortunately, the radiation was over quickly and we were soon free to go home. Lou never had any major side-effects and his spirits improved. He was soon his normal self. We were so happy to have him put the "sleepy time" behind him and enjoy life again. We were a family again although this time it was different.

We had been told that the radiation would not kill every cancer cell. The neuroblastoma would return. It was only a matter of time—6 months to a maximum of three years. The amount of radiation available for the next time he has brain symptoms would be less and less. The weapon of choice would kill the cancer but also kill the patient in the process. We asked ourselves: Would it make sense to do radiation even if it caused irreparable brain damage?

Fortunately, we had some time after the radiation was over. Mary Ellen and I talked endlessly about what to do and we both agreed on a strategy. It would be the most important decision of our lives.

CHAPTER 22: JULY TO DECEMBER 2003

July 23, 2003

Dear Friends and Family,

It has been a terrible few weeks for us. On July 2nd Louis developed a severe headache after playing in the pool for three hours. We took him to Yale for a work-up. The CT scan showed a large tumor in his brain. We were in shock. He had been doing exceptionally well up until that moment. We moved Lou to Sloan the next day for MRI and further work-ups. The tumor was diagnosed as a relapse of his cancer. On July 8th Lou underwent brain surgery to remove the tumor. The tumor was removed successfully without any neurological side effects from surgery. The neurosurgeon at Sloan did an amazing job and Lou's recovery was remarkable. He was talking and feeling good the next day and released from the hospital two days post-surgery. Follow-up scans showed that the cancer has spread to other parts of Louis's brain. This has caused Louis to become quite listless, although he is in no pain. We have finished the first round of chemotherapy and begin radiation to the brain and spine next week. The goal is to get the cancer under control. Life has been hard especially since Lou was doing so well with an "all-clear" only two months ago. We are overjoyed to have our son alive and well today and continue to cherish life one day at a time. Your prayers and good wishes are in even greater need now as we move forward with a new battle to get Lou back into remission.

Mary Ellen and I sat in the office with Dr. Kushner and Louis. He was upbeat with Louis while doing his usual checks, but he was more subdued with us. We discussed the long-term outcomes and the realities of radiation. We then told him that we had made up our minds on the next steps for Louis.

Louis was feeling well, his blood counts had rebounded since the transplant and although not anywhere near normal he could handle more treatment. Lou was ready and we were determined. We wanted to treat Louis as aggressively as possible to try to cure his relapse. We would not wait for the inevitable to happen and we wanted his help. We wanted to hear what he would recommend.

At this point in our lives we had come through the abyss of despair and were regrouping to continue our battle. We would never give up on Louis as he would not on us. He was a fighter and survivor. At 5 years old he had endured more than most adults would ever face. He was no quitter.

Once at home again, Mary Ellen took care of the boys, while I retreated to my office and buried myself in my old notes and the web. I had done research on relapses after we went to Chicago and had developed a list of websites that listed clinical trials for all kinds of cancer. It was actually simpler than I had thought. There was one central government website, ClinicalTrials.gov, which listed all registered clinical trials in the US. It has a simple search bar and as long as you type in the right medical terms you get a long list of experimental or early-stage treatments for your type of cancer. Sorting through the list is more difficult as many terms are in doctor-language and need to be translated.

I used the terms I had heard and written in my notes: neuroblastoma brain relapse, CNS (Central Nervous System) relapse, leptomeningeal disease, pediatric brain tumors, and more. Each search produced a long list of treatments, the more generic the search the longer the list, the more specific the shorter and more focused. This was my starting point and I soon had developed a way to scan the lists to find key words I was looking for—pediatric, CNS, neuroblastoma and brain.

I needed to attack this methodically. I set up an Excel spreadsheet with the following headings: Dr. Name; Phone; Institution; Description; Info. I typed in each trial that I felt was interesting based upon the description on the website. Here is a sample:

Doctor	Institution	Description	Info
Diller	Dana Farber	Temezolomide + Thalidomide	Could be done at Sloan
Warren	NIH/Baylor	Intrathecal Topotecan II	Results?
RN – Akin	NIH	Intrathecal Gemcitabine	Enroll Forms
Kramer	Sloan	Intrathecal 3F8 Antibody	Phase 1?
Friedman	Duke	Intrathecal Busulfan	Good Agent
Maris	CHOP	MIBG	No discussion yet
Balis	NIH	Intrathecal Mafosfamide	Good Agent

There were more than twenty trials on my list eventually. I visited numerous websites to double- check the trials. Noteworthy sites included these headings: "Clinical Trials for Brain Tumors," "Pediatric Brain Tumor Consortium," "Children's Oncology Group," to name a few. The wealth of information was remarkable and I absorbed all I could until my mind hurt.

Once I had assembled my list I decided to call all the doctors and ask for first-hand information about their clinical trials, the relevance to Louis's diagnosis, and any current results—since these were not usually published until years after the trial closed.

Basically, it was a three-day effort to call all the names on my list. Some of them I could not reach on a first try. I went back, and I went back, and I went back—I knew the research options. It was my son's life at stake. It was the ultimate challenge for any parent.

When doctors called back, and they all did, I took notes, and when I reviewed all the details on my spreadsheet, I noticed the word **"intrathecal"** had cropped up many times (at CHOP), the Children's Hospital of Pennsylvania in Philadelphia; at Baylor in Dallas, Texas; NIH, National Institute of Health in Maryland; and at Sloan Kettering in New York.

Dr. Name	Phone	Institution	Description	Info
Dr. Norris	Phone	Institution	Description	Info
Dr. Kramer		Sloan	Intrathecal 3F8 Antibody - 3 infusions - 14 cases	Wait 6 weeks post Radiation
Aleeda Akin - RN (nice)	301 496 0128	NIH	Intrathecal Gemcitabine - 03-C-0032	1 patient so far, lowest dose escalation now
Dr. Frank Balis - works with Blaney	301 796 4000 main	NIH	Intrathecal Mafosfamide - 90-C-0095	more patients
Cathy Warren	301 435 4683	NIH	Intrathecal Topotecan II 01-C-0123	Waiting for reply
Dr. Jason Farrar	301 894 1140	NIH	Temozolomide & 06 Benzylguanine	7/29 - will get back to me with best options
Dr. Gururangan	919 979 6923	Duke	Hi Dose Temozolomide with Stem Cell Rescue	7/22 contact and discussion
Dr. Friedman	919 684 5301	Duke	Intrathecal Busulfan	Will open soon - call if current treatment does not work
Dr. Lars Wagner	513 636 1846	Univ. of Cincinnati	Temozolomide & Irinotecan Phase 1 - could be done off study	Well tolerated - outpatient
			Utah & St. Jude's joint study	
Dr. Lisa Diller	617 632 3971	Dana Farber	Temozolomide & Thalidomide - could be done at Sloan - Phase 2	Message left on 7/23
Dr. Maris	215 590 2821	CHOP	Intrathecal Busulfan / MIBG - no discussion yet	Back first week of August - Make appt.
Dr. Audrey Evans	215 590 2250			
Dr. Susan Blaney	832 822 1482	Baylor	Intrathecal Gemcitabine - Vaccines	7/22 contact - Dr. Heidi Russell is also contact - no return call
Dr. Berthold	49 221 478 4380	Clinik Koeln	Advice	Send data
Dr. Susan Cohn	773 880 4562	Memorial Chicago	Post Radiation Intrathecal Topotecan - COG Study closed now	Dr. Kushner can access protocol and administer - Systemic treatment also necessary after some time
Dr. Cindy Schwartz	410 955 7385	Johns Hopkins	No call back	Call on 7/22
Dr. Matthay/Goldsby	415 476 3831	San Francisco	T8952 COG Trial Intrathecal Topotecan	Matthay on Vacation until Aug 5 - Dr. Goldsby to call me back
Dr. Victor Santana	(901) 495-2424	St. Jude's	Wed. call back	Back in the office tomorrow
Althea - asst.	901 495 3226			
Dr. Paul Sondel - Wisconsin			IL2, HU14.18Trial	no contact or info - NOT Eligible for Brain relapse??
Dr. Joanne Ater	713 792 6695	U of Texas	7/26 - No studies - nice lady - call her again when needed	Topotecan and Cyclophosphamide - systemic for relapse
Dr. Kolove	713 936 5892	Burzynski	Antineoplastons	

My working spreadsheet showing all of the clinical trials I had researched

Mary Ellen and I went through the list of trials and my findings. We both noted the trial at Sloan was open and seemed suitable for Louis. We decided that we would go wherever we needed to in order to give Louis his best chance. Now it was a matter of knowing what the best chance was.

This prompted me to make another urgent appointment with Dr. Brian Kushner. We agreed to meet as soon as possible. Dr. Kushner and I had developed a trusting and caring relationship over the past two years. I often emailed to ask him for test results or to provide help with issues Louis was having. He was always there for us and cared deeply about Louis.

He had battled neuroblastoma for twenty years and was always looking for new ways to get to higher survival rates and eventually a cure. If there was one doctor who would know all of the treatments on my list it would be Brian Kushner. I knew he would give me factual and frank advice about our options that I could trust.

Back in his office, I gave Dr. Kushner a copy of my spreadsheet and we went through every option, line by line. I was advocating in a way that I felt was the only way—presenting the science of all remaining options. He knew about all the trials, the respective doctors, and commented on all of them. One was not suitable, the next was an option, the next was too early, and the NIH trial looked promising until we got to the trial at Sloan Kettering.

We discussed the Sloan trial at length. It had not been used on neuroblastoma children yet, there were only 14 patients enrolled—all adults. We agreed that the 3F8 antibodies had worked very well in Louis's body and that it should, in theory, work in his brain. Dr. Kushner knew Dr. Kramer, who was overseeing the trial, well and had great respect for her. I could tell he was thinking about this carefully.

At the end of this arduous and taxing conversation Dr. Kushner said, "Well, that could, you know, could be an option. We are not really sure, that has only been for mostly adults. Let me talk to Dr. Kramer, let me get together a team, and let me figure something out."

Three days later, Dr. Kushner sent me an email. He had met with the team and they were working on a new protocol that Louis would be put on to treat his brain relapse. We were to come to New York the following week to go through it with him and meet Dr. Kramer.

Intrathecal is not an everyday word. "Theca" derives from the Greek, meaning a sheath or a shaft; and "intrathecal" describes the introduction by infusion of any substance into the layers of membrane that shelter the spinal cord and the brain. Two routes are used: a puncture to the spine, or a port in the patient's head called an **Ommaya Reservoir**.

As usual, I felt compelled to inform my online neuroblastoma community and this is what I said:

> *Mary Ellen and I decided that we wanted to treat Lou's relapse very aggressively, and not simply wait for the cancer to return at some point following radiation. We want to go after it now while it is in retreat. We decided to follow up the radiation with aggressive chemo followed by intrathecal, radio-labeled antibody treatment. The Intrathecal Phase 1 Sloan trial [to which the Sloan Kettering doctors have joined Louis Unger] attaches a*

137

radioisotope to the 3F8 antibodies, and infuses them directly into the spinal fluid through a port that Lou will have to have put into his skull (Ommaya Port). The treatment is experimental, and Lou will be the 15th person to undergo the Phase 1 study. It has low risks and gives us the best chance to destroy any remaining cancer that may be too small to detect. Cancer in the brain is still a mystery for the medical profession, although strides are being made in this area every day. The antibodies attach themselves to the NB and then release the radiation and kill the NB. As it is pinpoint radiation, instead of whole-brain radiation, no brain damage is expected. We are weaning him off the Decadron (Steroid to reduce brain swelling) which has made him gain 12 pounds and decreased his coordination. He is back to playing baseball and swimming and enjoying life. We will be doing scans in 3 weeks to see how Lou is progressing. Keep us in your prayers as we move into uncharted territory.

So we entered the world of phase 1 clinical trials. Clinical trials are research studies for desperate people who have nowhere else to turn for treatment. The medications used have already shown positive results in the laboratory, using mice, but have never been tried on a person. Clinical trials are conducted in a series of steps, called phases—each phase is designed to answer a separate research question. In phase 1, researchers test a new drug or treatment on a small group of patients for the first time to evaluate its safety, determine a safe dosage range, and identify side effects. If no adverse effects are present at a low dose, the dosage is increased until the side effects are too severe. The goal is to find an effective dosage that can be tolerated. In addition, the effectiveness of the new drug is evaluated.

Fortunately, the radiation treatments had worked wonders for Louis. He was feeling great, playing and enjoying life. Based on his condition it would seem almost insane to continue doing experimental and aggressive treatments. However, we knew that our son's condition was only temporary and that we had to act now to save his life.

Mary Ellen and I were ready even though we knew Louis would have to undergo additional hardships. First, an Ommaya port had to be surgically implanted into the top of his skull. This port was the gateway to

Lou's spinal fluid and was a requirement for the treatment. The procedure was done at Yale and was by all standards, routine. It left him with a small bump on the top of his head.

We knew Dr. Kim Kramer from the Clinic, where we had talked to her many times. She was a young, tall, and very personable doctor. She had three children of her own and her motherly instincts of kindness, love, and caring were a blessing. She had chosen a path that was hard to imagine. Within the field of pediatric oncology her goal was to find cures for the most difficult brain tumors. Her striking blue eyes and intensity revealed immense passion and unwavering dedication. Hers was a mission I found most noble and we were fortunate to be in her care.

Dr. Kramer described the treatment this way: "So we did the treatments, which meant admission to the hospital for careful monitoring during the infusion for a few days, then we did the intrathecal. He has this [Ommaya] port put into his head. He has a little bubble where they can just put the needle right in, goes right into the spinal fluid. Spinal fluid is clear, spinal fluid is not red, and it has no white blood cells. That's where you can get meningitis. If you get infections in your spinal area, you're gone, because you don't have any way to protect yourself. We take the 3F8, but because there are no white blood cells to attack and kill the mouse cells, they labeled the antibodies with radiation, and they infused those antibodies into the spinal fluid, and it finds the cancer cells wherever they're floating around, attaches itself, releases radiation, and kills the cancer cells in the brain and in the spine area. And Louis," Dr. Kramer recalls, "was one of three patients who got 3F8 at a higher dose level."

Along with 3F8—and this proved crucial— another antibody joined the fight, **8H9**, invented by Dr. Cheung, while trying to target neuroblastoma cells safely. 8H9 takes radioactive iodine into the spinal fluid where it only hits neuroblastoma, ignoring healthy cells. At Sloan, they call it "targeted radiotherapy."

So now, we had a small boy with a hole in his skull, and a needle sticking up out of it, while the radiation therapy poured into his head.

Understandably, we were nervous as the side effects of this experimental treatment could be serious.

Louis was taking it all in stride the bad cells were under attack once more.

Drawing of Lou with the Ommaya port being accessed – "I was in the hospital and had to get a needle in my head: 12-3-03"

During the infusion, they had a radiation officer present with a Geiger counter. It's very simple. They infuse it into his head and it just drips in. We didn't know precisely how his body was going to react. They proceeded with caution. There are two treatments of intrathecal 3F8. One is a pre-trial to monitor the severity of side effects. The pre-trial is not the full dosage—perhaps it was half a dose. The actual therapeutic dose was administered a week later

At times, I tried to imagine the antibodies floating around Louis's brain and hunting down the evil cancer cells. There were some in there for sure. When the 3F8 and 8H9 antibodies saw a bad cell, they chased it down while it tried to escape. The antibodies were so fast. They caught up and wrapped themselves around the neuroblastoma cells. Then, the tiny bit of radiation inside the antibody would be released, like a stealth missile, into the cancer cell.

The fight was short and sweet—the cancer cell died. Job done!

So, Lou was now undergoing the intrathecal treatment. We went into the pediatric ICU at Sloan for treatments. I truly believed this was going to save him.

CHAPTER 23: FIRST SURVIVOR

In mid-November on the northeast coast of the United States, it can be cold enough to see your breath and on a clear night, there will be a blanket of stars above you. Eleven years and four days after Louis Unger's first intrathecal treatment at Sloan Kettering, there were two dozen circles of powerful white lights, lighting up green Astroturf, a low steel fence, and many girls jumping about to keep warm.

Supportive parents were sitting on cold, steel bleachers.

There was an announcer, with a broadcast- quality voice asking trivia questions during breaks in the play: Who painted the Mona Lisa? To enthusiastic cheers from the crowd, a fit teenaged boy ran up a flight of concrete steps leading to the booth and received his trivia prize, a bag of candy. It was 6:30 on a Friday evening; the last football game of the season was in progress. It was a fierce game between local rivals—the Hornets in green were playing hosts to the Panthers in white. Mary Ellen and I were sitting on a rug on the freezing steel bleachers watching intensely.

The players varied in height; one was announced at six feet seven inches and weighed 240 lbs., as big as a refrigerator at seventeen years of age. It would have been possible to bring him down in a tackle, but only by tripping his ankles.

That night, he was likely to be taken down by a player who did not take his eyes off this giant, a much smaller fellow in green and white, who waited there like a bulldog for his moment to snap at the big fellow's ankles. This kid was on the field for much of the game, and at each snap he was right in the thick of it, beside the player with the ball, crouched and intent, waiting to do his bit. He was five feet four, a bundle of vitality, sharp as a tack. He was sixteen years old, and his name was Louis Unger.

When he first took to a sports field that Friday night, Mary Ellen saw a face across the field that she recognized—the oncologist whom she had last seen when the woman was telling her in Yale New Haven Hospital that Louis had a major brain tumor. That evening, although their sons were playing on opposing sides, both mothers cheered for Louis.

Lou after a football game for Hamden Hall – he played nose tackle

This protocol is technically known as the "General cRIT-based treatment plan for patients with relapsed CNS NB." Dr. Kim Kramer published the 104 week-long treatment plan in the National Institute of Health, J Neurooncol Manuscript in May 2010 entitled, "Compartmental Intrathecal Radioimmunotherapy: Results for Treatment for Metastatic CNS Neuroblastoma."

Most impressive in the write-up is the survival chart published as an attachment. Before Louis's protocol, all kids with a brain relapse survived for no longer than three years. This 2010 chart shows a horizontal line that stretches out to nearly six years. The survival percentage of the children on the line is at 80%.

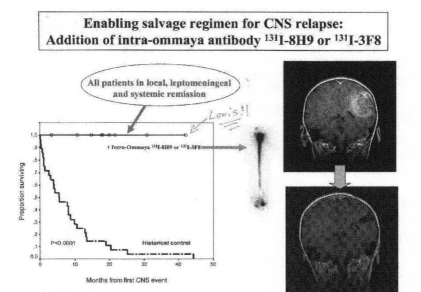

**Enabling salvage regimen for CNS relapse:
Addition of intra-ommaya antibody ^{131}I-8H9 or ^{131}I-3F8**

All patients in local, leptomeningeal and systemic remission

Lou's!!

+ Intra-Ommaya ^{131}I-8H9 or ^{131}I-3F8

P<0.0001

Historical control

Proportion surviving

Months from first CNS event

The "Unger Protocol" chart published in 2010 – Lou is the first circle!

When reviewing this book, Dr. Cheung informed me that the number of patients on this protocol has grown even beyond Neuroblastoma children and new statistics will be published soon showing the 10 year survival rate at 60%. This means that 60% of children that had Louis's devastating brain relapse and were treated with the "Unger Protocol" are now surviving. What used to be zero percent chance of survival is now 60%.

When Mary Ellen and I look at the simple chart (from the 2010 publication) we are forever thankful that the first tick mark at the very end of the chart that represents one special patient, Louis. Approximately seventy children and counting are now long-term survivors thanks to this breakthrough treatment.

We will always remember our last meeting with Dr. Kushner in March of 2008. Louis was then 10 years old and had just finished another round of tests. It was almost 6 ½ years since Thanksgiving 2001.

We had been looking at various options to prevent a relapse. Our aggressive treatment philosophy had gotten us this far and we were not sure what would be next. After checking Louis as he always did, Dr. Kushner said something we did not expect—actually it took us by complete surprise. He said: "There is no need to come back for further treatments or testing. We believe you're cured."

We were stunned. Could this be true? We made Dr. Kushner repeat what he just said. Yes, he was sure that Louis was cured!

CONCLUSION

The word "breakthrough" is not used lightly here. A breakthrough typically involves: an offensive assault; moving beyond an obstacle; a sudden advance in knowledge; or a notable success. All of these definitions apply to the story about Louis.

There were breakthroughs by doctors, parents, and by Louis himself.

At the very beginning of this crisis, the late Dr. Diana Beardsley at Yale broke through her usual reach to stretch far beyond, and take as much care of Louis as she possibly could. Dr. Beardsley had every right to step away from this case on the grounds that as a nationally recognized hematologist, she pursued disciplines that were at best tangential to cancer. Yet she took on the case. She provided a level of care and excellence outdone only by a hospital like Sloan that specializes in children with this form of rare cancer. In addition, she broke another barrier—she kept my wife and I totally informed all the time. She answered our every question. This was not the norm.

It's clear that Dr. Gregory Germain, Lou's pediatrician, also practiced giving us information and advice every step of the way. He believes that keeping parents highly informed helps a young patient heal. Since he is now Associate Chief of Pediatrics at Yale Children's Hospital, he has been able to make his beliefs more widely practiced.

"Since Louis," he has said, "we have greatly improved communication. In fact, families round [consult] with all the specialists now. Right at the child's bedside. It's called **Family Centered Rounds**," and it has made a huge difference in patient safety and the patient experience. There are patient surveys that command actual change in real time.

Patient advocates travel the hallways. There are morning "safety huddles" that address and solve each of the prior day's errors or near errors. Patients have iPads at their bedside that give them updated information such as vitals and lab tests. They give the patient a new and immediate communication tool with their physician and nurse. What Mark and Mary Ellen Unger did on their own initiative has become the standard of care."

Sloan Kettering, for its part, knew it had a breakthrough when Brian Kushner's and Kim Kramer's adjusted, targeted protocol began to work on Louis Unger. Such a moment! Twenty-five years of disappointment, endless trials, failure after failure until this success. This case created a new pathway, a new "road-map," to use Dr. Kramer's term.

At reunions and fundraisers, the doctors from the neuroblastoma team meet more and more survivors every year, and provided the child is referred to them in time, they can now claim to have raised the survival rate from a general fifty percent to a more typical number somewhere between sixty to seventy-five percent.

These days, patients with neuroblastoma relapses in the form of a brain tumor—depending when the patient presents—can be cured. Previously, the survival rate had always been a firm zero. In other words, there are many children today who might not be alive had Louis Unger not been assaulted by neuroblastoma. So, that is another momentous breakthrough.

Mary Ellen and I consider the education we received to be a breakthrough, too. We found strengths and abilities we didn't know we had. We had never advocated for a young patient before and we broke through a few barriers!

Traditionally in the West, there were rigid barriers between doctor and patient or patient's family. Timidity yielded to authority; anxiety bowed to formality; the white coat ruled. My personal style of relentless inquiry and Mary Ellen's style of devoted mothering combined to burst through the walls of stultifying tradition. The doctors did not see us as critics or adversaries; instead, we became a valuable part of the team delivering the very best care to a young patient fighting for his life.

We were so far ahead of our time. Patient advocacy has now evolved and become an educational add-on to every hospital stay. Back then, for anyone to question the traditional system priding itself on objectivity, for parents to present their own research results for potential treatments, for parents to offer observations, and to push to the point where a leading doctor, admittedly a man of extraordinary kindness and dedication, responds and weighs in, such as Brian Kushner—well, that was some important groundbreaking!

Louis with Dr. Kushner at a Band of Parents charity event 2017

Here is the last mass email I sent out with an update on Louis:

January 29, 2006

Dear Friends and Family, During our recent meeting with

Lou's oncologists at Sloan Kettering we were expecting to discuss the next steps in his treatment plan. A special plan that has been crafted by the talented team of neuroblastoma experts for Louis's brain relapse.

When Lou relapsed with a large brain tumor in July 2003, the prognosis left little room for hope. No other child had survived this type of relapse. Here we are 30 months later and Louis is doing great.

Through our work together with the best doctors in the world, we crafted a new roadmap for Louis and he has trail-blazed it with his usual courage and good spirit. As we sat in the office anticipating a discussion on another round of experimental treatment, the doctor said - We think Louis does not need any more treatments! We were speechless.

What an amazing feeling! Mary Ellen and I could not

believe it. Amazingly, Lou now has a treatment protocol named after him at Sloan for kids who have a similar relapse to Louis's. There are now other kids, just like Lou who are following in his path and also doing well. Lou is truly a miracle.

We can only imagine that a combination of all the people who have prayed for Louis, coupled with doctors who have the courage to try new things, and the love of his family have gotten us to this point. After all the treatments Louis is doing great at school, playing sports, and battling his brother at every turn. We are so very proud of him as he has been a beacon of strength throughout all of his torment. We are cautiously optimistic for the future and will now try hard to get back to a normal life for all of us. Thank you all for your thoughts and prayers - they have helped us make it through a treacherous road.

Every day is a great day. Love,
Mark, Mary Ellen, Harry and Louis

We now live at the end of a long, curved driveway in a house that can't be seen from the road. Having moved there ten years ago, as Louis was beginning to recover, both sides of the driveway are now showing the beautiful benefits of Mary Ellen's landscaping. Hank, our black Labrador, has a tail that can bruise your leg when he wants to show how happy he is to see you.

From this calm, private position, it's almost impossible to imagine that families and children are still going through the agony and turmoil that we went through. They are. We have not forgotten all the super-human people we met, nor the countless kindnesses. We are happy to think we have made a positive and lasting difference to that world.

In the mind of every parent who has ever had a neuroblastoma child, one question appears like a hologram: Can it be cured? Dr. Nai-Kong Cheung, of his own admission, still thinks about little else.

"I'll tell you how I define 'cured.' When my patients get married and have children, that's cured, isn't it? That's all I can expect. And it's happening now. To me that's such an incredible feeling. There's still a lot that's unknown, no question. But at least life goes on. That to me is the beauty," said Dr. Cheung.

A proud moment – Lou's high school graduation – 2015

Life goes on for Louis Unger. Today, Louis is a living, breathing, smiling breakthrough all in himself, a boy of immense charm, from whom a sense of fun is never distant which is astonishing, considering what he has endured. He's thoughtful, engaging, quick-witted, sociable, and eager to contribute. His brother, Harry, is a fierce supporter of Lou and could not be more proud of him. It makes me proud to hear him speak of his brother:

"Louis has always had a tendency to milk every opportunity he gets. If I stole a toy from him, he would use that to leverage my parents months after the fact. To this day, he will try to blame a bad report card, or losing a race, on the things he's gone through. And though I respect and admire what he did, I will not cut him any slack. He's been given a rocky path to follow to becoming a man, but I know it's one he can follow. Every time he tries to give an excuse for a failing, it's like he falls back a step. That's where I step in as his older brother. I can't help him climb that path, but I'll be damned if I'm going to let him fall back down."

Lou will never fall back down. His effervescent nature won't let him, and his upbeat personality obscures any trace of the ordeals that he has endured. He has no memory of being afraid. His early childhood memories are classic. He watched animal programs, tormented his older brother when he tried to enjoy television, and played with little, plastic dinosaurs. When asked if he remembered being afraid, he said, "No, because I honestly wasn't told the fact that I was going to die. A life-or-death situation? I was never told that. I was always occupied with something. I guess you could say that I was very optimistic, because I was always like, "Oh, let's get this over with now so I can go back to playing.

"I remember, I think I got addicted to pain medicine which made me feel really good: sleepy, happy, and warm. And then after the medicine wore off, my mom always told me that I had a very sour attitude, very bad temper."

He's aware that his illness and multiple hospitalizations have given him something that his peers cannot even begin to fathom.

"I do want people my age to try and understand what I've gone through: being stuck with a needle; having the IV attached to a pole; and being confined to a hospital bed. Things happened that they'll never understand, because they'll never know what it's like," he has said.

At school he's taking a class on forensic science, and he reads across a wide range. Under the eye of an English teacher whom he admires, he's been through Death of a Salesman, Hemingway, and The Great Gatsby;

"I think The Great Gatsby is a great book. My teacher said there's not a word in there that shouldn't be in there. It's brilliant. It's sad but it's true. It's about a guy, who goes after a woman, and the woman got another guy, and he doesn't accept that."

Lou is about to do a term paper on one of the major war books, The Things They Carried by Tim O'Brien. It's a visceral story of the Vietnam War; and he's about to read Deliverance. Such an edgy reading taste could be taken as traced back to the trauma he himself has been through, and out of which he has emerged with extraordinary maturity. I asked him what he says to people facing surgery or hospital and he said, "There are some people that actually have come to me for tips, and so I say, 'Be co-operative, be nice to the doctors, because they're just there to help you. Not trying to inconvenience you in any way. And make sure you smile a lot. Make sure you know it's worthwhile. It's not like being held in a jail. You're being held but you're free. You'll be a pretty lucky guy, that's one thing. Second is you'll have an experience that many people don't have, and it will make you look differently on life'."

When pressed for a longer description of what he remembers about his illness, Lou describes an impression of a long, ongoing series of treatments and procedures, with his mother managing him from one treatment to the next using a series of rewards:

"The first time I ever got a videogame console was when she said, 'If you do this treatment we'll get you a videogame console.' The thing is, I didn't even know what I was doing all the treatment for. I was kept under a test, one after another. It didn't really mean anything to me. I mean, I didn't even know if I'd die or not. It wasn't clear. It wasn't something I thought of. A three-year-old doesn't think of whether he's going to die or survive, it's not something he should be confronting."

To look at Lou today is to marvel: How many punctures in his skin? How many needles? How many pounds of chemical drugs coursed through him? How many scans spread under space-age machines, trying to please everybody by lying absolutely still? How might any human of any age come through all of that without some emotional lesions?

"It certainly made me regret some things. I might have been taller; I'm only five foot four or something. And sometimes it's always on my mind, wondering what would it be like if I didn't have cancer at all. You know—why me? That's something I always think—why did this happen to me? That's what I'm still trying to figure out."

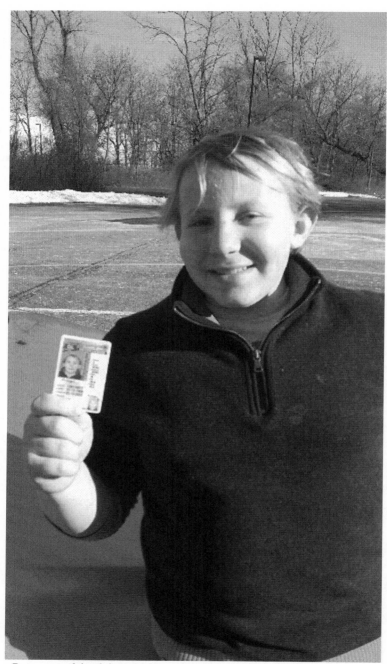

Lou gets his driver's license on his 17th birthday – 2015

GLOSSARY

8H9 is a protocol that takes radioactive iodine into the spinal fluid where it only hits neuroblastoma, ignoring healthy cells. At Sloan they call it "targeted radiotherapy." The radiolabeled form of 8H9 received "Breakthrough" designation from the FDA in June of 2017.

A.L.L Acute Lymphocytic Leukemia, also called acute lymphoblastic leukemia, is a cancer that starts from the early version of white blood cells called lymphocytes found in the bone marrow.

A.M.L. Acute Myeloid Leukemia is characterized by the rapid growth of abnormal white blood cells that build up in the bone marrow and interfere with the production of normal blood cells.

Ativan is a benzodiazepine. It works by slowing down the movement of chemicals in the brain. This results in a reduction in nervous tension (anxiety) and causes little sedation.

adrenal glands are endocrine glands that produce a variety of hormones including adrenaline and the steroids aldosterone and cortisol. They are found above the kidneys.

Adriamycin, also called Doxorubicin, is a chemotherapy medication used to treat cancer. It can cause nausea, mouth sores, loss of appetite, stomach pain, diarrhea, hair loss, and heart damage.

advocacy is an activity by an individual or group which aims to influence decisions within a specific environment such as a healthcare.

afebrile means without fever.

anemia results from a lack of red blood cells or dysfunctional red blood cells in the body. This leads to reduced oxygen flow to the body's organs. Symptoms may include fatigue, skin pallor, shortness of breath, light-headedness, dizziness, or a fast heartbeat.

anesthesiologists are medical professionals who provide medical care to patients in a wide variety of (usually acute) situations, including preoperative evaluation, consultation with the surgical team, creation of a plan for the anesthesia tailored to an individual patient, airway management, intraoperative life support, and pain control.

antibody therapy uses a person's natural immune system functions to fight cancer.

aspirate To aspirate is to remove a fluid from a body cavity using an aspirator—a tool with suction such as a syringe.

Ativan is a benzodiazepine. It works by slowing down the movement of chemicals in the brain. This results in a reduction in nervous tension (anxiety) and causes some sedation.

Bactrim is a brand name for an antibiotic. The generic names for this medication are sulfamethoxazole and trimethoprim

Benadryl is a brand name. It is an antihistamine that blocks the effects of the naturally occurring chemical histamine in the body.

biological markers are the measures used to perform a clinical assessment. A "favorable" marker indicates the high possibility of survival; an "unfavorable" the opposite.

biopsy The removal of cells or tissues for examination by a pathologist. The pathologist may study the tissue under a microscope or perform other tests on the cells or tissue. There are many different types of biopsy procedures. The most common types include: (1) incisional biopsy, in which only a sample of tissue is removed; (2) excisional biopsy, in which an entire lump or suspicious area is removed; and (3) needle biopsy, in which a sample of tissue or fluid is removed with a needle.

blood-brain barrier (BBB) The brain is the only organ known to have its own security system, a network of blood vessels that allows the entry of essential nutrients while blocking other substances. Unfortunately, this barrier is so effective at protecting against the passage of foreign substances that it often prevents life-saving drugs from being able to repair the injured or diseased brain.

bone marrow transplant A bone marrow transplant is a procedure to replace damaged or destroyed bone marrow with healthy bone marrow stem cells. Medical shorthand calls it BMT, and in the place of cells that have been damaged by cancer and chemotherapy, fresh cells are planted back in the cleansed bone marrow. From these, healthy new cells can grow. It's complex and expensive, and it's considered if cancer remedies, such as chemotherapy drugs, have damaged or annihilated normal stem cells when chemotherapy alone is working.

bone scan A bone scan is a test that can find damage to the bones, find cancer that has spread to the bones, and watch problems such as infection and trauma to the bones. A bone scan can often find a problem days to months earlier than a regular X-ray test.

Broviac is a trademarked name for a catheter. A catheter, or an implanted port (Port-a-Cath), places a central line into a large vein and can be used to administer medication directly into the bloodstream. Blood samples for labs can be withdrawn without repeatedly inserting a needle through the skin and into a vein.

cancer is a group of diseases involving abnormal cell growth with the potential to invade or spread to other parts of the body.

Carboplatin is a chemotherapy medication used to treat a number of forms of cancer.

CBC is a complete blood count (CBC) is a blood test used to evaluate overall health and to detect a wide range of disorders, including anemia, infection and leukemia.

Cisplatin is the generic name for an anti-cancer ("antineoplastic" or "cytotoxic") chemotherapy drug. It can destroy cancer cells, has a platinum base, and may cause loss of hearing.

clotting Coagulation (also known as clotting) is the process by which blood changes from a liquid to a gel.

control (in a clinical trial) is a group of subjects closely resembling the treatment group in many demographic variables but not receiving the active medication or factor under study. The control group serves as a comparison group when treatment results are evaluated.

crystallization is a technique which chemists use to purify solid compounds.

CT Computed tomography (CT) is a diagnostic imaging test used to create detailed images of internal organs, bones, soft tissue, and blood vessels.

Cyclophosphamide (CP), also known as cytophosphane, is a medication used as chemotherapy to suppress the immune system.

Decadron is classified as a corticosteroid (more precisely a glucocorticosteroid), and has many uses in the treatment of cancer. It is a steroid that helps with falling platelets, but can cause stomach upset, dizziness, insomnia, increased appetite or weight gain.

diagnosis A diagnosis is the conclusion that is reached following examination and testing of a patient.

Dilaudid is an opioid pain medication.

Doxorubicin is a synthetic chemotherapy drug also called Adriamycin. It affects the bone marrow, and can cause nausea, mouth sores, loss of appetite, stomach pain, diarrhea, heart damage.

embryonic stem cell is an immature cell that can be directed to become any kind of cell that the body needs.

Emla cream is a local anesthetic (numbing medication) containing lidocaine and prilocaine. It works by blocking nerve signals in the body. It is a cream that eases severe burning, stinging, or sensitivity where the medicine is applied to the skin and the needle inserted.

endoscopy is a procedure that allows a doctor to view the inside of a patient's body. An endoscope often has a channel so the doctor can insert tools to collect tissue samples.

ER Emergency room

Etoposide is a chemotherapy drug derived from the mandrake plant, usually known as the mayapple, and indigenous to North America, Etoposide causes, among other things, loss of hair, also caused by other drugs. Indeed they all come with side-effects ranging from the unpleasant to the dangerous.

family-centered rounds is a model of communicating and learning between the patient, family, medical professionals, and students on an academic, inpatient ward setting.

ganglion is a mass of nerve tissue existing outside the central nervous system.

ganglioneuroblastoma is a rare tumor that forms in nerve tissue and is often located in the abdomen. These tumors are mainly found in children under age five.

ganglioside is a molecule composed of a glycosphingolipid with one or more sialic acids linked on the sugar chain.

GCSF is a drug used to stimulate the production of granulocytes (a type of white blood cell) in patients undergoing therapy that will cause low white blood cell counts. This medication is used to prevent infection and neutropenic (low white blood cells) fevers caused by chemotherapy.

growth hormone is made in the pituitary gland which stimulates the release of another hormone called somatomedin by the liver, thereby causing growth.

hematologist is the specialist concerned with the study, diagnosis, treatment, and prevention of diseases related to blood.

hemoglobin is the part of blood that contains iron, carries oxygen through the body, and gives blood its red color.

Ifosfamide is a chemotherapy drug that attaches to DNA in cells and may kill cancer cells.

Immunology is the branch of biomedicine concerned with the structure and function of the immune system.

intrathecal is a way to deliver drugs with an injection into the spinal canal, or into the subarachnoid space so that it reaches the cerebrospinal fluid (CSF) and is useful in spinal anesthesia, chemotherapy, or pain management. This route is also used to introduce drugs that fight certain infections, particularly post- neurosurgical. The drug needs to be given this way to avoid being stopped by the blood brain barrier.

intravenous means into or connected to a vein.

irradiation is the application of radiation such as X- rays for therapeutic purposes.

kidney stones are hard objects like small stones that sometimes form in a kidney and that can cause great pain.

Kytril is a drug used to prevent nausea and vomiting that may be caused by medicine given to treat cancer.

Legg-Calvé-Perthes is a childhood hip disorder initiated by a disruption of blood flow to the ball of the femur called the femoral head. Due to the lack of blood flow, the bone dies (osteonecrosis or avascular necrosis) and stops growing.

leptomeningeal means having to do with the leptomeninges, the two innermost layers of tissues that cover the brain and spinal cord.

leukemia is a group of cancers that usually begin in the bone marrow and result in high numbers of abnormal white blood cells. These white blood cells are not fully developed and are called blasts or leukemia cells.

ListServers is a small, electronic program that automatically redistributes e-mail to names on a mailing list. Users subscribe to a specific mailing list.

lymph nodes are small, bean-shaped structures that are part of the body's immune system. Lymph nodes filter substances that travel through the lymphatic fluid, and they contain lymphocytes (white blood cells) that help the body fight infection and disease.

lymph is a transparent, usually slightly yellow, often opalescent liquid found within the lymphatic vessels, and collected from tissues in all parts of the body.

lymphomas is cancer of the lymph nodes.

malignant In regard to a tumor, having the properties of a malignancy that can invade and destroy nearby tissue and that may spread (metastasize) to other parts of the body.

marrow is a soft fatty substance in the cavities of bones, in which blood cells are produced

mass In medicine, a mass is an abnormal growth of tissue resulting from uncontrolled, progressive multiplication of cells and serving no physiological function.

mediport A catheter connects a mediport to a vein. Under the skin, the port has a septum through which drugs can be injected and blood samples can be drawn many times, usually with less discomfort for the patient than a more typical "needle stick". Ports are used mostly to treat hematology and oncology patients.

Mesna is a drug used to prevent damage to the urinary tract of people being treated with the anticancer drugs cyclophosphamide or ifosfamide.

metabolic is the result of all the processes in your body working together to create the energy that keeps you going.

metastases To spread from one part of the body to another. When cancer cells metastasize and form secondary tumors, the cells in the metastatic tumor are like those in the original (primary) tumor.

MIBG is a nuclear scan test that uses injected radioactive material (radioisotope) and a special scanner to locate or confirm the presence of pheochromocytoma and neuroblastoma, which are tumors of specific types of nervous tissue.

monoclonal means forming a clone that is derived asexually from a single individual or cell.

3F8 monoclonal antibody is a drug derived from the white blood cells of baby mice. When 3F8 is infused into the body it binds to the outer surface of Neuroblastoma cells like a magnet. When the body detects these antibodies it sees them as a foreign body and determines that they need to be killed. The body then unleashes its own immune system to destroy the mouse cells and with it the Neuroblastoma cells.

MRI Magnetic resonance imaging (MRI) is a technique that uses a magnetic field and radio waves to create detailed images of the organs and tissues within your body. Most MRI machines are large, tube-shaped magnets.

myeloablative describes a type of high-dose chemotherapy that kills cells in the bone marrow, including cancer cells. It lowers the number of normal blood-forming cells in the bone marrow, and can cause severe side effects. Myeloablative chemotherapy is usually followed by a bone marrow or stem cell transplant to rebuild the bone marrow.

nadir, in the context of cancer, means the moment in chemotherapy when the red and white blood cell counts drop to their lowest.

neuroblastoma "Neuro" comes from the Greek word, neuron, meaning originally a sinew or a cord, and then, when it went into Latin as nervus, it mutated to mean "nerve" as in "nervous system." At the other end, -oma came from crops and vegetables, and was used in the antique world to describe something that had taken root, and formed a growth or a tumor. Medicine took hold of the suffix and used it to describe a condition of tumors. The "blast" in the middle of the word has nothing to do with "gust of air, usually hot," as most dictionaries offer; it comes from Greek, the word "blasthos" and it means a bud or a sprout, something immature, something not yet fully grown, in which context it is used by the medical and scientific communities.

neutropenia is the presence of abnormally few neutrophils in the blood, leading to increased susceptibility to infection. It is an undesirable side effect of some cancer treatments. When testing for neutropenia, the laboratory takes its measure from a component of the white blood cell, the neutrophil, and the lab generally rates parameters based on an absolute neutrophil count (ANC). In adults, the ANC ranges between 1,500 and 8,000 microliters of blood, and anything along that scale constitutes a perfectly safe reading. Next step down - mild neutropenia stands between counts of 1,000 and 1,500, and at that level the possibility of infection remains slight, though rising.

nuclear scan Nuclear medicine scans can help doctors find tumors and see how much the cancer has spread in the body (called the cancer's stage). They may also be used to decide if treatment is working. These tests are painless and usually done as an outpatient procedure.

Ommaya Reservoir is a device surgically placed under the scalp and used to deliver anticancer drugs to the fluid surrounding the brain and spinal cord.

oncology is the study of cancer. An oncologist is a doctor who treats cancer.

orthopedist An orthopedic surgeon, a physician who corrects congenital or functional abnormalities of the bones with surgery, casting, and bracing.

pediatrics is the branch of medicine dealing with children and their diseases.

platelet is a small colorless disk-shaped cell fragment without a nucleus, found in large numbers in blood and needed in clotting.

pluripotent is an adjective describing an immature cell capable of differentiating into one of many cell types pluripotent stem cells

portacath In medicine, a port is a small medical appliance that is installed beneath the skin. A catheter connects the port to a vein.

prognosis is a forecast of the likely course of a disease or ailment.

propofol is a prescription sedative-hypnotic drug (brand name Diprivan) that is administered intravenously. Propofol is commonly used in the induction of general anesthesia and can be used both for the induction and maintenance of general anesthesia.

protocol The term used for a treatment program, the American Medical Association defines the word as "an official account of a proceeding; especially the notes or records relating to a case, an experiment, or an autopsy; and/or a detailed plan of a scientific or medical experiment, treatment, or procedure." (It derives from a Greek word protokollon, meaning the first page or the flyleaf of a document outlining its contents; proto- meaning first and -kollon from a word meaning "glue," because the flyleaf with its list of progressive content was glued to the rest of the book.)

In other words, a protocol, as the COG applies the term, lays down a series of steps, whether surgical, pharmaceutical or both, to be followed when seeking the best results in the treatment of pediatric cancer.

radiation therapy uses high-energy radiation to shrink tumors and kill cancer cells. Radiation therapy can either damage DNA directly or create charged particles (free radicals) within the cells that can in turn damage the DNA. Cancer cells whose DNA is damaged beyond repair stop dividing or die.

radiologists are medical doctors (MDs) or doctors of osteopathic medicine (DOs) who specialize in diagnosing and treating diseases and injuries using medical imaging techniques, such as x-rays, computed tomography (CT), magnetic resonance imaging (MRI), nuclear medicine, positron emission tomography (PET) and ultrasound.

randomize A study in which people are allocated at random (by chance alone) to receive one of several clinical interventions. Participating in a randomized controlled trail usually means one group receives a pretend treatment (placebo).

relapse is the return of a disease or the signs and symptoms of a disease after a period of improvement.

remission A decrease in or disappearance of signs and symptoms of cancer. In partial remission, some, but not all, signs and symptoms of cancer have disappeared. In complete remission, all signs and symptoms of cancer have disappeared, although cancer still may be in the body.

Stage Four Cancer A cancer is said to be in stage 4 when it has spread far away from the origin into other organs of the body, this progression is also known as metastasis and unless a metastasis is singular— meaning that it has only spread in to one specific location—and it's still accessible, it usually means that the cancer will no longer be curable with localized therapies such as surgery or radiotherapy.

stem cells are cells with the potential to develop into many different types of cells in the body. They serve as a repair system for the body.

superior vena cava is a large vein that receives blood from the head, neck, upper extremities, and thorax and delivers it to the right atrium of the heart.

tramadol is sold under the brand name Ultram among others, and is an opioid pain medication used to treat moderate to moderately severe pain. When taken as an immediate-release oral formulation, the onset of pain relief usually occurs within about an hour.

transfusions A blood transfusion is a routine medical procedure that can be lifesaving. During a blood transfusion, donated blood is added to your own blood. A blood transfusion boosts blood levels that are low, either because your body isn't making enough or you've lost blood owing to surgery, injury or disease.

tumor is a swelling of a part of the body, generally without inflammation, caused by an abnormal growth of tissue, whether benign or malignant.

Vancomycin is an antibiotic used to treat a number of bacterial infections.

vein a tube forming part of the blood circulation system of the body, carrying in most cases oxygen- depleted blood toward the heart.

Vincristine is a chemotherapy drug originating in ingredients taken from the vinca or periwinkle ground cover plant, causes constipation and hair loss, and can induce abnormal nerve pain, aggressive pins and needles, in the hands and feet.

X-rays are a quick, painless test that produces images of the structures inside a body—particularly bones.

Zofran is used to prevent nausea and vomiting that may be caused by surgery, cancer chemotherapy, or radiation treatment. It is a serotonin-based drug and, in some instances, it can cause blurred vision, or slow down the heart rate; contrariwise, it can also promote anxiety, and it can dry the nasal passages and throat.

A CONCISE HISTORY OF SURVIVAL

1	Thanksgiving 2001	stage 4 neuroblastoma diagnosis: Yale
2	Nov 2001	1st round of chemo
3	Dec 2001	2nd round of chemo
4	Jan 2002	move to Sloan Kettering: Dr. Kushner
5	Jan 2002	3rd round of chemo
6	Feb 2002	1st round of 3F8 antibodies (5 days)
7	Feb 2002	tumor removed. broviac catheter inserted.
8	Feb 2002	4th round of chemo
9	Mar 2002	2nd round of 3F8 antibodies (5 days)
10	Mar 2002	5th round of chemo
11	Apr 2002	3rd + 4th round of 3F8 antibodies (10 days)
12	Apr 2002	no evidence of disease (NED)
13	May 2002	stem cell harvest
14	May 2002	bone marrow transplant with stem cell rescue (30 days)
15	Jun 2002	positive bone marrow test for neuroblastoma
16	Jul 2002	5th + 6th round of 3F8 antibodies (10 days)
17	Jul 2002	no evidence of disease (NED)
18	Jul 2002	radiation of spine and skull

19	Aug 2002	7th + 8th round of 3F8 antibodies (10 days)
20	Sep '02-Feb '03	monthly rounds of 3F8 antibodies (30 days) + oral chemo
21	Jul 2, 2003	brain tumor relapse
22	Jul 2003	surgery to remove brain tumor
23	Jul 2003	radiation of spine and skull
24	Aug 2003	chemo targeting brain with stem cell rescue (5 days)
25	Nov 2003	surgery to insert Ommaya port into skull
26	Dec 2003	1st round of intrathecal radio- labeled 3F8 antibodies (test dose)
27	Dec 2003	2nd round of intrathecal radio- labeled 3F8 antibodies (full dose)
28	Feb '04-Apr '04	monthly rounds of 3F8 antibodies (30 days) + oral chemo
29	Jul 2004	Make-A-Wish trip to Wyoming to dig for dinosaurs
30	Feb '05-Jun '05	monthly rounds of 3F8 antibodies (50 days)
31	Aug 2005	1st round of intrathecal radio- labeled 8H9 antibodies (test dose)
32	Aug 2005	2nd round of intrathecal radio- labeled 8H9 antibodies (full dose)
33	Mar 2008	Louis declared cured.

MEDICAL BACKGROUND

The word **antibody** came into play toward the end of the nineteenth century as the bounty hunter to "antigen." In the shortest of shorthand, an antigen is anything that the body's immune system considers foreign, a threatening interloper. To counter such an intruder, the body generates—or is given by immunization or other means—a protein to kill the specific intruder, an anti-body.

Bone marrow is in general the factory where the living organism, man or beast, manufactures blood cells. Each blood cell comes from a stem—hence "stem cells," the youngest, the most immature of all. (Important note: stem cells also exist in rich abundance within the blood of the umbilical cord, which is why far-seeing parents have them harvested at the birth of a child.) As a stem cell ages, it gives rise to a white cell, a red cell, or a platelet. Given a chance to mature, the cells that came from the stem cells in the bone marrow will divide, and only then do they become more susceptible to the chemotherapy drugs. (White cells circulate and live for twelve hours before dying off; red cells live for weeks; platelets for several days.)

When the mature cells retire after a few days, the body's defense systems will eventually succumb to the chemo, and when they do, the blood count falls to the lowest recorded point—the nadir. Hospital staff manage the calendar, to control the timing of chemotherapy dosages, so that the stem cells are not damaged while they are actually producing their healthy, maturing cells. When the blood counts indicate the nadir, it means that the body's defenses against infection have bottomed out, and the watchfulness must increase. Due to low platelet count, there will be little or no clotting agent in the blood vessels; thus a simple cut could cause problems right up to hazard levels.

Chemotherapy doesn't only attack cancer cells, it also hits healthy cells—in fact, it strikes at everything. When chemo causes the drop to the nadir it triggers the widespread effects on hair, mouth and nose mucus, intestines, the red and white blood cells, and their all-time helpers, the platelets, that come from the bone marrow and swarm to the rescue in the event of damage to blood vessels. (Under a microscope, platelets look like little plates.)

There is, however, an arena where damage is limited, where

167

destruction of cells by chemo is slower to happen – in the bone marrow, that inner, sponge- mushy substance that you can see in the core of a meatbone.

G-CSF (Granulocyte-Colony Stimulating Factor) is delivered by injection, and is a protein. A granulocyte is a type of white blood cell that the bone marrow produces.

In 1986, at the age of 77, Rita Levi- Montalcini, an Italian neurobiologist, won the Nobel Prize for discovering something called "growth factor," present in all healthy bodies. Vitamin B12 is a growth factor, so is insulin. G-CSF is an applied growth factor that acts on the bone marrow to increase the production of certain white blood cells. It's used during chemotherapy, when white blood cells are under attack, to help maintain white blood cell production, and thus to obviate something called "neutropenia" —a perilously low white cell count (Greek word, penia, meaning poverty).

When the body is weakened by acute illness, a G-CSF—or any such injection—can sometimes cause a problem, such as a rash near the injection point. The protein itself can make the recipient feel heavy, with deadening pains in the bones; fever can also descend. If tolerated, though, G-CSF will become a positive force; by stimulating the growth of white cells, it may even help to reduce the duration of the nadir.

Neuroblastoma is a condition where, in (neuro-), the nervous system, immature cells (-blast) form tuberous growths (-oma). These cells explode like microscopic fireworks all through the body, and unlike maturing cells, do not remain where they should belong. (In all cancers the rogue cells form masses that damage nearby structures such as organs.) With neuroblastoma, these clustering, multiplying immature nerve cells bunch together and make tumors. Mainly this cancer attacks young children (though adults can contract it too), and when found in a fetus is often called a "neuroblast." Most doctors use a shorthand, "N-B," and it has been mistaken for a form of leukemia.

The first major, incontrovertible symptom of a neuroblastoma is an unusual growth or lump that can happen just about anywhere in the child's body. A common location is the adrenal gland, where between a third and a half of all pediatric neuroblastomas begin. From their little perch next to each kidney, the adrenal glands, part of the sympathetic nervous system, act as control aids, most commonly known for their call into action when danger, excitement or stress come roaring in, or with the famous "three F's"—Fright that leads to Fight or Flight.

If a doctor presses on a child's abdomen and the child winces in pain that calls for scrutiny. If there's a mass, depending on where the tumor may be pressing, there can be numbness or pain.

If there's a neuroblastoma pressing on the spinal cord, it can paralyze, and the doctor will observe the child's restricted movements. If the tumor is large enough, it can actually be seen as a bump on the surface of the body, protruding from a bone, or the neck in the case of lymph nodes.

If there's neuroblastoma in the skull and the tumor is large enough, it will even protrude from the skull and eye sockets to look like an egg or a sphere on the top or the side of the child's head. If it begins to affect where it has spread, it can produce other physical, observable evidence — for example, it will cause a fractured thighbone, or bulging eyes, and even complaints of "I can't see."

Neuroblastoma is not new. German doctors came up with the first tentative definitions in 1864, and expanded upon them in 1891, but the breakthrough work was carried on by three early twentieth-century physicians. In 1901, William Pepper at the University of Pennsylvania described a version of Neuroblastoma Stage or Type Four in very young children. For a number of years, the condition when detected in the adrenal gland and/or a heavy spread into the liver had the name, Pepper's Syndrome.

Six years after Pepper's first announcements, Robert Grieve Hutchison at the Hospital for Sick Children in London reported the involvement of the skull bones—then it became Hutchison's Disease.

In 1910, James Homer Wright at Massachusetts General Hospital tied the package together by naming the tumors "neuroblasts," because he had identified the connection between the tumors arising from adrenal glands, and the immaturity of the cells in affected fetuses and infants. Some of his discovery occurred by way of autopsies determining why children had died.

Over the years, doctors have called neuroblastoma "the Enigmatic Disease," because its ways are so frequently mysterious. They report cases where a large tumor in an infant has been removed surgically, and that ended the matter – no metastasis, and therefore no treatment needed. Louis Unger had the polar opposite; he had a tumor that was racing, spreading and metastasizing—which is the great fear, because it means that the cancer is moving here there and everywhere, and very possibly too late to be treated and subdued.

In 2001, children with Stage One and Stage Two neuroblastoma had a ninety per cent chance of surviving. At Stage Three it came down to around sixty per cent; at Stage Four, the level Louis had, the chances of his survival within five years of his first diagnosis were, as Dr. Beardsley indicated, statistically around twenty to thirty per cent. According to all medical knowledge and experience, he had close to an eighty per cent likelihood of dying by the time he was eight years old.

Back in the 1960's, Ayub **Ommaya**, a Pakistani neurosurgeon, invented a way of releasing medication directly into the elixir of life itself, the spinal fluid.

The **Ommaya port** sits beneath the surface of the skull, accepts chemotherapies, antibodies, and antibiotics, and sends them, on their mission of healing, down a tube into a basin deep within the head, where the all-important cerebrospinal fluid is produced, and from where it flows up around the brain and the spine. (This reservoir can also be used for extracting fluids.)

The independence of the device allows higher concentrations of chemotherapies that go straight to the spine and the brain, bypassing the blood-brain barrier. In fact, when sending in radiation tagged to an antibody, the dosage can be high enough to warrant the presence of the hospital's Radiation Officer. Side effects tend to be limited to temporary fever an nausea.

The term **Patient Advocacy** suggests difficult possibilities for doctors, and because in many cases it does cause friction, wide areas of medicine have been wary of it. The more enlightened medics, though, take a different view. Dr. Richard O'Reilly, former Head of Pediatrics at Sloan Kettering, is very much in favor of it and said this: "I think that parent advocacy is a really critical variable. The degree to which the parents are engaged, asking questions, working for their children—that's a continuing stimulus. On another level, I think that parent advocacy has also increasingly become united in this country. So you're having groups like the Band of Parents, and several other parent groups that will get together and say, "What can we do to help?" And that has also been a major force, particularly in this time when NIH funding has been much more limited. They've been a major force helping to foster research."

Perthes or **Legg-Perthes** takes its name from the three orthopedic surgeons who identified it a century ago; Arthur Legg, an American; Jacques Calvé, a Frenchman; and a German surgeon named Georg Clemens Perthes, who first tracked what he considered a degenerative disease in children's hips and limbs. Fifty children in a million suffer from it between the ages of three and ten. It's half a dozen times more common in boys than girls, and it's often confused with or dismissed as "growing pains."

Stage One: This stage is usually a small cancer or tumor that has not grown deeply into nearby tissues. It also has not spread to the lymph nodes or other parts of the body. It is often called early-stage cancer and is highly curable, usually be removing the entire tumor with surgery.

Stage Two and Three: These stages indicate larger cancers or tumors that have grown more deeply into nearby tissue. The cancer may have also spread to lymph nodes but usually not to other parts of the body. Treatment will normally require surgery, chemotherapy and today immunotherapy (antibodies)

Stage Four: This stage is the most severe form of cancer diagnosis, where the cancer has spread to other parts of the body, such as bones, organs, the brain, etc. It is also called advanced or metastatic cancer and is treated with the most advanced and severe tools available today. Louis Unger was diagnosed at age 3 with Stage Four Neuroblastoma.

RESOURCES FOR SUPPORT

ACOR LISTSERV (Association of Cancer Online Resources)
is a unique collection of online cancer communities designed to provide timely and accurate information in a supportive environment. It is free lifeline for everyone affected by cancer & related disorders. (This site is being replaced rapidly by closed groups on social media such as Facebook.)
www.N-BLASTOMA@LISTSERV.ACOR.ORG

Children's Neuroblastoma Cancer Foundation is a private foundation that provides information and support for Neuroblastoma families.
P.O. Box 6635 Bloomingdale, IL 60108
www.cncf-childcancer.org

The Children's Oncology Group (COG), a National Cancer Institute supported clinical trials group, is the world's largest organization devoted exclusively to childhood and adolescent cancer research The Children's Oncology Group (COG), a National Cancer Institute supported clinical trials group, is the world's largest organization devoted exclusively to childhood and adolescent cancer research.
www.childrensoncologygroup.org/

ClinicalTrials.gov is a registry and results database of publicly and privately supported clinical studies of human participants conducted around the world. It is an easy to use database where you simply type in the name of the disease and are lead to a large listing of all the trials for the disease. An excellent resource for researching available treatments.
www.clinicaltrials.gov

Facebook is now one of the leading social media platforms and it has many resources available to those afflicted with many types of ailments. Many groups on Facebook are closed as users must apply to join these groups. But application and approval are normally swift and the peer to peer information can be extremely useful. Facebook is now one of my first recommendations for those looking for information to go.

Make A Wish Foundation (Connecticut). Tens of thousands of volunteers, donors and supporters advance the Make-A-Wish®vision to grant the wish of every child diagnosed with a life-threatening medical condition. There is a Make a Wish office in almost every state in the US. **www.wish.org**
Elsevier Science B.V
Sara Burgerhartstraat 25
P.O Box 211, 1000 AE Amsterdam The Netherlands

Memorial Sloan Kettering Cancer Center. One of the leading cancer treatment centers in the world. It has a specialized team of doctors and surgeons that focus exclusively on the advanced treatment of Neuroblastoma. Louis is alive today due to the fine doctors at this institution. **www.mskcc.org/pediatrics/cancer-care/types/neuroblastoma**

Pubmed – Is a large database of many published medical articles comprised by the US Government's National Medical Library and Institute of Health It comprises more than 28 million citations for biomedical literature from MEDLINE, life science journals, and online books. It takes some patience and often a medical dictionary (ie: google) to read through research papers from leading doctors and is another valuable resource.
www.ncbi.nlm.nih.gov/pubmed

National Institute of Health (NIH), part of the U.S. Department of Health and Human Services, is the nation's medical research agency — making important discoveries that improve health and save lives. The NIH often has its own clinical trials and research that is easily accessible online. We had signed up for an NIH trial for Louis when he relapsed with his brain tumor but opted to be treated at MSKCC.
www.nih.gov/

Neuroblastoma
G.M. Brodeur, T.Sawada, Y. Tsuchida and P.A. Voute. First Edition 2000

Neuroblastoma

N.K. Cheung and S.L. Cohn Springer 2005.

Pediatric Brain Tumor Consortium
A Multidisciplinary cooperative research organization devoted to the study of correlative tumor biology and new therapies for primary CNS tumors in children
www.pbtc.org

PubMed comprises more than 27million citations for biomedial literature from Medline
www.ncbi.nlm.nih.gov/pubmed

SuperSibs powered by Alex's Lemonade Stand
Siblings often get overlooked if a brother or sister are diagnosed with cancer. This organization has special events and activities geared toward the siblings to help them cope.
https://www.alexslemonade.org/campaign/supersibs

What is Neuroblastoma, A Handbook for Families
Children's Hospital at Richland Memorial Columbia South Carolina

ABOUT THE AUTHOR

Mark Unger was born and raised in Solingen, Germany, where his mother and father started a manufacturing business — a place famous for its cutlery. In 1978 the family moved to Weston, Connecticut. He graduated from Weston High School in 1984 and then attended Babson College in Wellesley, Massachusetts. After working in the shipping industry for three years he joined his family business in 1992 and married the love of his life, Mary Ellen Delaney in 1994.

Harry, their first son, was born in 1996 followed by Louis in 1998. The family was confronted with Louis's diagnosis of neuroblastoma, a rare and deadly childhood cancer, on Thanksgiving day 2001, when he was three years old. The battle to save Louis's life and the incredible medical breakthrough that saved their son created a burning desire for Mark to document his unique story.

By learning how to confront the complex medical world his family had been thrown into, Mark and his wife were forced to overcome adversity. By engaging in their son's new world of modern medicine they learned how to advocate for their son and overcome the diagnoses of "zero chance of survival." Mark hopes this book will help other families engage in their treatment and strongly advocate for their loved ones who are facing medical hardships.

Mark and his family live in Bethany, Connecticut. He is a Director and Owner of his family business, Unger Global, and active in a number of charities. Mark enjoys travelling with his wife to explore new places, playing golf, fishing and riding snowmobiles.

Made in the USA
Middletown, DE
31 July 2020